RECLAIMING OUR REPUBLIC

An American Utopia Within Your Grasp

Jack Cullinane, MBA MS

-------Dubesor & Co-------
Baltimore

Edited by Kyla M. Cullinane
Published by Dubesor & Company
Baltimore, Maryland
www.dubesor.com

Second Paperback Edition
ISBN: 979-8-9929687-3-6
Printed in the United States of America

First, this book is dedicated to my father, a man of supreme intelligence, stalwart principles, and strong work ethic, who has fallen through every crack in the fabric of society but who perseveres to give us love, happiness, and wisdom.

Secondly, I dedicate this new edition to Nick Stewart for rising to this moment and giving me a shot to be the action I preach of.

Forever grateful.

Table of Contents

Preface i
Foreword iii

-Part One - A Declaration of Purpose

When the Elm Turns Gold 3
Introduction 13
The Vision for a Principled Republic 17
What If I Just Don't Care? 25
Government Shmovernment: Who needs it? 29
Why democracy tho'? 33
Equitable Leadership 37
On Liberty and Its Responsibility 41
On Morality and When Government Should STFU 47
American is Multicultural; sry, not sry 51
On Race in America 57
On Shutting Up about Free Speech 59
When States' Rights are Right and Wrong 63
The Pragmatism of Separating Church and State 69
Data and the Final Frontier 73
Comments on All the Commas in Politics 77
MAGA: The Dystopia Within Our Grasp 81
Our Best Weapons: Compassion and Peace 85

-Part Two- An Action Plan

Alex Surmises 91
Pathways to Progress 93
The Prosperity Economy 97
Media and Social Media 107
Foreign Policy 113
Healthcare 119
Immigration 125
Education 131
Gun Rights 137
Criminal Justice Reform 141
Energy and Climate Mitigation 147
Government Debt and Finance 151

-Part Three- Words to Action

Without a King 157
Isn't it too late? 159
A Note on the Future of Humanity 163
What You Can Do 167
To the Politicians with Love 172

Acknowledgements 177
End notes 179

RECLAIMING OUR REPUBLIC

An American Utopia is Within Your Grasp

Preface

Perhaps the sentiments contained in the following pages are not yet sufficiently fashionable to procure them general favor. A long habit of not thinking a thing wrong gives it a superficial appearance of being right, and raises at first a formidable outcry in defense of custom. But the tumult soon subsides.

Time makes more converts than reason.

-Thomas Paine, ***Common Sense*** 1776

•

Cages or Wings? / Which do you Prefer? / Ask the birds / Fear or Love, baby / Don't say the answer / Actions speak loud than words. /

What does it take to wake up a generation? / How can you make someone take off and fly? / If we don't wake up and shake up the nation / We'll eat the dust of the world / Wondering why.

-Jonathan Larson, ***Tick, Tick... Boom!*** 1990

Foreword

Si ignis in populo non est, solus in culpa sum

When I first released *Reclaiming Our Republic,* I carried with me the vague hope that a single book—raw, imperfect, but deeply earnest—could save America. I sometimes called it "the shitty little book that could save America." I believed ideas, plainly spoken, might cut through the noise.

I learned quickly how difficult that is. It is hard to make a book resonate in a fractured country. I poured myself into TikTok videos, speaking to thousands. I sent the book to political leaders. One Baltimore County candidate invited me to work on his campaign because the message struck a chord. Congressman Kweisi Mfume, my own representative, wrote me back with words that gave me strength: he called the book inspiring, and said we need more leaders willing to take bold stands.

Those encouragements were real. But as months passed, reality set in. I came to see just how deep the divide truly runs. The differences in this country are not cosmetic—they are structural. We are living through an unprecedented era of disinformation, division, and corrosion of principle right as the world is at a critical inflection point of climate change and a new geopolitical order. The question before us is no longer whether we should act—it is whether we will act boldly enough to meet the moment.

In these pages, I employ an allegory. At the center is an elm tree—chosen for a reason. The elm represents the core fabric of America: Equity, Liberty, and Morality (E - L - M). If that tree dies, everything within it suffers.

The creatures in the allegory represent us. The ants are the workers, the middle and lower classes who labor tirelessly, too often unheard. The bees are the white-collar workers, civil servants, writers, engineers, academics, and educators—the ones who keep the hive of society alive with constant effort. The birds are the leaders: politicians, celebrities, journalists, and influencers, those whose reach extends beyond the elm. And then there is the hummingbird—small, different, feeding from the same flowers as the bees but moving in another way. The hummingbird is the messenger, the bridge, the one who awakens others to the truth.

Against them comes the locust. The locust represents Donald Trump, the MAGA movement, Project 2025, and the anarcho-capitalist oligarchs now devouring our institutions. The locusts pretend to belong to the ecosystem, but their presence spreads plague. They do not nurture the elm; they consume it. One important point, the locusts are not necessarily those who voted for Donald Trump. They are not the coal workers of West Virginia or the farmers of Iowa. The locusts are not the millions of people who voted once or twice for this regime. Those are good people who have been given bad cards, bad information, and worse leaders. If you are among them, you have a choice. Even those that believe in Locusts have a choice: same choice as the rest of us.

Here is the lesson of my story: the hummingbird cannot save the elm alone. The ants, the bees, the birds—all must rise together. That is the choice before us. We cannot merely discuss ideas; we must act on them. Action will look different for each of us, but action is required.

In publishing the first edition, I also learned a sobering truth: some Americans no longer believe democracy itself is worth saving. There is no such thing as an ordinary election anymore. This is not an episode of *The West Wing*. This is a crucible moment in human history. We will either preserve liberty and equity through principled leadership, or we will watch our republic fall into the ashes of authoritarianism as so many civilizations have done before us.

I do not believe collapse is inevitable. History moves toward greater freedom, greater prosperity, greater understanding—when we have the courage to claim it. But progress is never automatic. It requires leaders who can see past the false dichotomies of left and right, who can call the nation back to principle. It requires each of us to see past the false dichotomies of left and right and call ourselves back to principles. We are our savior—we are the leaders.

Our problem is not a lack of solutions. Our problem is leadership. For decades, Americans have voted for politicians who promised change but deepened division. Donald Trump and his imitators offer the illusion of solutions but only produce destruction. They will survive that destruction, the rest of us will not. But most Americans, I believe, still hold to equity, liberty, and morality. Most of us want families to succeed, children to prosper, peace to endure, opportunity to be real. Nobody votes for despair.

Even those like Charlie Kirk or Stephen Miller who hold deeply bigoted and divisive views. When you boil down their rhetoric it is only fear. They see society collapsing just like we do. But their solution is a king. Their solution is to whitewash the past, the present and the future with fearmongering, violence and hate. That is not the American way and that's not a solution. It's been tried throughout history, and it fails every single time. Tyranny is a band-aid for a sick land. Compassion, liberty and equity are the kinds of things that heal civilizations.

The beauty of the American experiment has always been that ordinary people hold the power to shift the winds of history. That remains true. If you dislike the government you have, you have the right and responsibility to change it. If you believe in equity, liberty, and morality, then now is the time to act.

This book does not claim to have every answer. My framework may not be the approach that ultimately prevails. But what matters is that we begin the conversation, that we choose action over apathy, and that we demand principled leadership of ourselves and of our republic.

We are entering a dark chapter. But we have been here before. We can choose to let this darkness consume us, or we can be the generation that lights the way to the next horizon.

The republic is still ours to reclaim. Let us take it.

- PART ONE -

A DECLARATION OF PURPOSE

When the Elm turned Gold

Once upon a time on a flourishing hill stands a stalwart elm shining in the summer sun. It is home to many creatures. All living in relative harmony. These many creatures each have their own particular place in the society of the elm. The Robins and Jays are the heralds and singers. Keeping the creatures informed and entertained. The ants do much of the hard labor of the elm. They build and dig and move and sort all the things the creatures need and make. The bees weave together the society of the elm. They organize and cultivate the many industries of the elm. They venture out along with the birds to pastures around the elm to acquire anything the society needs for its welfare.

Together these creatures are captains of their fate. There are certainly problems that confound the society of the elm. Sometimes the birds seem to take more than their share. Storms may ravage the elm causing damage. Regardless of these troubles and any resentments they may create among the creatures, they are united in their shared purpose to care for the elm tree. The efforts of the creatures ensure the tree is nourished, its damage is healed and continues to grow. Such is the exquisite harmony of the society of the elm—a balance of individuals united by a shared love of their home and dedicated to its longevity and wellness for all.

Perched upon a skyward branch is a humble hummingbird named Alex. Alex is an inquisitive little bird. A sharp hummingbird known for his industrious nature and fine Verdun feathers. Alex has been of the society of the Elm since he hatched. It is his home, and he loves it dearly. From upon his perch Alex sees his prey. He launches, wings flittering at immense speed. He zooms at a direct angle downward. The wind rushes through his fine feathers. Too soon, he has to slow down and comes to hover in front of his target: a bright flower blooming in the pastures that surround the elm. Alex patrols these pastures and knows them well. As a Hummingbird he navigates these same pastures as the bees but holds a different view. He will travel further and explore more than the bees who tend towards the routes and areas they know best.

On more than one occasion, Alex had discovered new sources of nectar or supplies for the great elm—or warned of potential issues from his explorations.

One day, after finishing his work among the blooming flowers, Alex flew back to his perch high atop the elm. From there, he noticed something strange on the horizon.

As far as the eye could see stretched green pastures and healthy trees. But on this day, far in the distance, some trees looked sickly and dark. Their leaves were turning a yellowish gold, their branches blackening. He had seen such decay before, but never so far and wide. Then, to his astonishment, one of those distant trees collapsed—blackened and gold, withering into dust. From its remains, small creatures rose and took flight. They weren't birds or bees, or any species Alex had seen before. He couldn't tell what they were, only that they were strange.

When Alex descended to the nesting area to report his findings, Herbert Bee was there to receive his day's harvest.

"Good day to you, Herbert," said Alex. "I found plenty of nectar today. But I also saw something peculiar on the horizon—a black and gold tree fell over. Have you ever seen such a thing?"

Herbert buzzed cheerfully. "Can't say that I have, can't say that I have. No complaints, no complaints."

"I'm not complaining," said Alex, "but it seemed strange."

"Hmm," Herbert replied, and went back to sorting pollen. That was the way of the bees—they never complained. They simply buzzed along and got the work done.

After turning in his nectar, Alex flew home. His neighbor, Riley Robin, greeted him warmly.

"Hey, Alex! How are you today?"

"I'm well," Alex said. "Though I saw something strange—a black and gold tree fell. Never seen one fall like that before."

Riley shrugged. "Ah, not to worry, not to worry. Tragic, sure, but such things happen. Poorly man-aged forests, most likely. The jays think we should send help to them, but I say one less tree means more for us, right?"

"But what about the creatures that came out?" asked Alex. "I saw them flying away. They weren't birds or bees."

"There are many creatures in the world," Riley said, unconcerned. "I'm sure they're harmless. I wouldn't worry."

Alex noticed that Riley always ended conversations that way—I wouldn't worry. Sometimes he found it amusing; today he simply nodded and went home.

About a week later, Alex was sitting upon his perch high on the elm. He was given a special assignment from Herbert that day: he needed a particular kind of nectar. So Alex searched high and low and started to fly out, making circles around the pasture seeking the kind of flower that he needed. And he saw off in the not-so-far-distance, among the pasture, a set of creatures he'd never seen before.

He perched along a bush and watched them from afar. They were strange-looking, with six legs. They were longer than a bee, but flew in a sort of haphazard way among the bushes and trees. They were golden in color, matching the sunlight as it faded beyond the horizon. And he saw that if they stayed too long in a particular tree or bush, it started to wither away. They seemed to kill whatever was near them—but not quickly. The flowers were still good; it was just the roots around them that seemed to wither away.

He watched these creatures for a while. He saw them each day around the outer edges of the pasture. One day, as he sat upon a bush, he was greeted by his friend, David the Jay.

"Alex," David said, "greetings! What do you seek? Can I help you out?"

"Oh, David, no, I'm good. I'm working on a quota for Herbert. But I noticed these creatures out over there—you see them? They're the golden ones. Any idea what they are? They seem to do something to the roots of some of the plants. I've noticed they started to die over there."

"Oh," said David. "Yes, I know them. They're the locusts, yes. Some trees end up having them. They come and they take advantage of the plant in every way. The plant survives for a while, but eventually it just dies off. I've seen it before—some of the far-off lands, far-off trees, way away."

"You ever seen them this close?" asked Alex.

"No, I've not," said David. "But I wouldn't worry much. They've never come to our elm, and we do quite well. They're attracted to a sickly plant, someplace that's already beyond the pale, so to speak. Then they move in. Our elm is strong, so I'm sure we won't have a problem. I wouldn't worry."

Alex noticed as well—every time he talked to a jay, they always said, "I'm sure it's not a problem. I wouldn't worry."

"Okay," said Alex. "That's fine. Well, I'm done with my break. I'm off and away."

Alex took off, and David called after him, "Well, let me know if I can help in any way."

About a week later, Alex was in his nest, resting after a long day's work. Sometimes he liked to look deep into the branches of the elm just to see if anything was happening. He saw on this day, high up in the top branches along the outskirts, a locust perched very near where he sometimes sat.

He was alarmed. Never before was a locust there. He flew up and spoke to it.

"Sir, I've never met you before. You've never come to our elm, is that right?"

The locust said, "No, no. I've been here all along. We've always been around the elm. We're eve-rywhere."

"And what do you do, sir?"

"Oh, we make everything better. We help keep everything alive."

"Really? I've seen you around in other pastures, but it seems like some of those plants died when you were around them."

"Oh, we do what we can," said the locust. "But there are parasites among the plants in these pas-tures which we attack. We try to root them out, but sometimes there's only so much we can do."

"There are parasites here?"

"Oh yes, absolutely. There are parasites everywhere. We try to help whenever we can. Have you seen these parasites?"

"No, I have not," Alex said.

"Well, be on the lookout for them," said the locust. "If you ever see some, make sure to let us know. We will come, eat them, and remove them so everyone may be healthy."

"Okay, thank you," said Alex, and he flew off.

Over the next few months, more and more locusts appeared around the elm. The elm was abuzz with talk of these parasites the locusts had described. The robins and jays continued to say, "There is nothing to worry about. There is surely not a problem."

Then one day, Herbert came to Alex looking distraught.

"They don't need me anymore," Herbert said quietly. "The locusts have taken over the supply work. They say there are parasites in our nectar."

Alex was stunned. "But that's what they say?"

"That's what they say," Herbert buzzed. "Who am I to say otherwise?"

Little by little, the locusts took over more creatures of the elm. And little by little, one day, as Alex was making his patrols, he noticed golden streaks along some of the leaves on the outer reaches of the elm. He flew down to the base, thinking maybe there were parasites. But there was an entire colony of locusts that had taken over the interior of the trunk.

He flew down near them and watched, but once the locusts saw him, they flew out at him, yelling obscenities, calling him a parasite. Alex flew fast and dodged around, hiding among bushes in the pasture.

Eventually, the locusts went away.

He kept searching around. He started to notice it was harder to find flowers because throughout the pasture there were locusts, and the pastures began dying. Fewer and fewer flowers came up.

The birds continued to say on a daily basis, "There are no worries. There are no issues. Have no concerns."

But Alex began to be concerned because he could no longer gather. He was not meeting his quotas.

One night, Alex sat with Herbert, who coughed and wheezed. Alex had searched all day for the medicine that would help his friend, but he couldn't find anything.

"I'm sorry, Herbert," Alex said, "I have tried."

Herbert said, "No complaints. I've done what I could. I think it would have been better had the locusts not come. Perhaps the parasites sickened me, but I hope they can get rid of them soon."

Alex said, "I don't think that's true."

But he watched as Herbert's life slipped away. The bee buzzed one last time and stopped moving.

Alex was sad. He went back home and saw David there talking to Riley.

When Alex told Riley and David, Riley only repeated, "Perhaps the parasites got him. Thank goodness for the locusts."

David disagreed. "No, it is something else. It can't be the parasites. We must have another problem"

Alex became angry. "We've seen this before—trees turning gold, trunks blackening, then falling to dust. The locusts claim to save them, but they're the cause."

Riley protested. "Bees die all the time. You're overreacting. Give it time. When the locusts are done, the elm will flourish again."

But soon even Riley fell ill, coughing like Herbert had. Alex pleaded with her. "Come with me. We'll fly to the far meadow—the one untouched by locusts."

"It's dangerous," Riley gasped. "If we leave, we might spread the parasites."

"There are no parasites!" Alex cried. "If I die saving you, so be it." He lifted her with his wings and carried her through the fading light to the untouched pasture. There, amid thriving flowers, Riley's strength returned.

"See?" Alex said softly. "The only difference here is that there are no locusts."

Riley looked around, wonder in her eyes. "You may be right. I don't want you to be, but you are. Thank you, Alex."

"Now we must save the others," he said. "We need to remind everyone what the elm once was—how we thrived before the locusts ruled everything. We'll spread the truth, you and I, and David too. We'll remind them of who we are—and we'll sing it until everyone remembers!"

Introduction: No Unsolvable Problem

Amid the creases of our national soul, we believe in a persistent truth that with liberty, equity, and morality, we can guide ourselves towards prosperity. The United States was built by a group of individuals who rejected authoritarian rule and divine right as the foundation for governance. Instead, they believed that at the heart of a just society lies the fundamental right of individuals to make decisions for themselves, for their families, and for their communities. They held that, as a collective, humans possess the ability to determine what is best for themselves.

We recognize the need for leaders who unite us into a common vision for the future. However, there are those who seek to claim leadership to enrich themselves through manipulation and exploitation rather than to serve the greater good. These individuals, driven by greed and ambition, perpetuate the lies that permeate our society. They tell us that poverty is inevitable, crime is always rising, and that society is always on the brink of collapse. They argue billionaires create the economy, healthcare is a privilege, and that violence and discrimination are facts of life. These narratives instill fear, division, and helplessness into society, presenting a distorted view of reality to maintain power.

The truth is much simpler. There are no unsolvable problems in this country. The real enemies we face are not shadows in a "deep state" or an amorphous blob of brown people from abroad. Instead, we have powerful and greedy people who wish to maintain their wealth and influence. They are the ones who benefit from perpetuating division. Meanwhile, there are millions of us feeling lost or desperate after experiencing generations of trauma and change. We are unsure of where to turn next because there are no leaders who seem willing to do the work. Our leaders seem increasingly sycophantic and dysfunctional. The American people deserve leaders at every level of government who approach solutions with morality, equity, and liberty; the same principles upon which this nation was founded, but which have been overshadowed by apathy, greed, and corruption.

Until we, as citizens, take it upon ourselves to become the founding fathers of a new path, our nation will remain adrift. There is a common ground between the most liberal and the most conservative among us. Within each of us, we can recognize that all Americans, regardless of their beliefs, background, or political affiliation, want the same things: the chance to make their lives better and to ensure that their children can do the same. We all seek safety in our homes, protection from external threats, and the freedom to live without being exploited. We all want access to healthcare and opportunities for prosperity, and above all, we want a country where our personal dignity and autonomy are respected.

We are at a turning point. If we take these principles to heart, hold our leaders accountable, and unite for the common good, we can build a society where the values we aspire to are not only ideals, but realities for all.

The Vision for a Principled Republic

It is impossible to reflect on modern society without an abject sense of doom. The world seems to be falling backwards into old dogmas, basic fears, and the same tyrannies of our forefathers all while facing existential threats unique to human history. In the face of this, I declare that there's a better path which offers a future of prosperity instead of doom.

Most people view utopia as an impossible dream that, like perfection, can never truly be attained. But maybe utopia could be the stage of civilization where equity, liberty and morality are the foundations of daily life. In such a society, every individual would have purpose, value, and inalienable rights. Certainly, utopia includes the abolition of poverty and the guarantee that no one faces undue persecution. We love to pray for and hope for world peace, but human nature appears incompatible with literal world peace. Perhaps harmony and non-violent compromise are achievable. In this sense, utopia is not a perfect nation, but instead it is an imperfect society that operates on universal principles like equity and morality with fairness, liberty, and dignity. To me, that vision feels attainable because that fits the image of a United States that lives up to its ideals.

Historically, ideologies like communism have attempted to create utopianism through the violent overthrow of the "elites." This has never worked. Instead, over the last couple of centuries, capitalist democracies have created incredible wealth and prosperity, yet they too fall short of this utopia. The reason for this failure is that our society has been hijacked by unprincipled oligarchs while we have been maligned and massaged into apathy and vanity.

The core problem within American politics today is that the political establishment has become disconnected from coherent values and principles. Terms like democracy, freedom, and equality have become muddled and misunderstood due to their overuse and misapplication. Words like communism and socialism have been so warped by history and propaganda that their original meanings are lost. When discussing political ideas, much has been lost in translation. Take the example of conservative thought in the United States. Historically, the conservative ideal has been to limit government power and give more authority to individuals and businesses. Yet, on issues like abortion, conservatives argue for government intervention while arguing against government control for guns, vaccines, and deadly pollutants. This presents an unaddressed paradox in the conservative brain. The doublethink creates a psychological ecosystem where truth is a matter of faith not fact which fuels immoral rationalization and social division. Even still, this absurdity is not limited to conservatives. Liberals have long argued for a bigger government to manage social programs and welfare, yet they advocate for less government intervention for issues such as abortion and marriage.

The rise of Donald Trump exemplifies this disconnect. The MAGA Oligarchy does not have a philosophy or a platform. Instead, it is a personality cult which claims goals of semi-fascist reform while working towards the endgame of kleptocratic revolution (Think Russia in 1990s). Indeed, for years, the Republican Party has increasingly become a vehicle for greed and white Christian conservatism, without articulating a comprehensive vision for society. The Democratic Party, too, lacks a clear set of values, often offering opposition to Republican policies without presenting a coherent vision of its own, preferring amorphous tropes like hope and change. In this political vacuum, the need for a new, alternative vision becomes apparent—something beyond the hollow, personality-driven politics that dominate today. To that end, I have created this framework of a principled republic which seeks to establish a generation of leaders who fight for universal prosperity using a foundation of equity and objective morality.

I believe there are fundamental moral principles that most people can agree on—things like helping the sick, not killing others, and taking care of children. These values are central to human existence and form the foundation of society. At its core, morality is about taking care of one another, ensuring that people have good lives, and acknowledging the inherent importance of existence itself. Being kind, avoiding exploitation, and treating others with respect are integral norms to a healthy society and to a universal moral framework. To achieve any level of utopia, our politics must emphasize these basic moral values which means having leaders that are willing to make tough decisions based on a universal morality.

The principle of objective morality offers a structured methodology for solving problems[i]. Objective morality can be defined as a data-driven approach that seeks to minimize exploitation and maximize equity for the least privileged. At the heart of this approach is the identification of the least privileged in any given situation, as they are the ones who stand to gain the most from interventions aimed at improving equity.

In this context, equity refers to fairness in opportunity and outcomes by acknowledging that not everyone starts from the same place. In a race, everyone may travel the same distance, but not everyone starts from the same starting line. While every human is equal in dignity and rights, the circumstances of an individual's birth—such as their geography, bio-demographics, or socioeconomic background—are not equal. Yet these factors impact the course of the person's life substantially. Material wealth is a paradox of diminishing returns. For the richest people, an increase of 10% in their wealth is unlikely to be transformative because there are only so many material possessions or experiences one can enjoy. Meanwhile, if an impoverished person receives a 10% increase in wealth, that can feel very substantial. Undoubtedly, 10% of a billion is greater than 10% of 30,000. But, speaking from experience, when you have to decide which bill gets pushed to next month so that you can get groceries, $250 more per month is a big deal.

The real power of equity lies in lifting those at the bottom of the social ladder. By improving the lives of the least privileged, the whole of society benefits because more opportunities are created for everyone. This stands in contrast to the story we are told about how wealth naturally flows from the rich to the poor. In reality, the rich have no reason to redistribute wealth to the poor. This is why modern governments exist rather than feudalism. By focusing on equity, leaders can provide a moral system for individuals while also ensuring that the entire economic system works more efficiently and sustainably for everyone, including the wealthy.

One of the core tenets of objective morality is the minimization of exploitation. Exploitation occurs when a more powerful party takes advantage of a less powerful one, extracting benefits at their expense. Exploitation can take many morally reprehensible forms including the exploitation of people, ecosystems, cultures, and power structures that all create circumstances that disadvantage the silent and less powerful. By minimizing exploitation, objective morality ensures that any given solution to a societal issue is morally sound while preventing the creation of new injustices. These goals are why empirical evidence is the other core tenet of objective morality. Without a solid empirical foundation, decisions may fail to address the issues at hand or worse exacerbate them. Making decisions without empirical evidence or without understanding the potential risks involved is not only impractical but unethical and irresponsible.

In practice, objective morality posits that political and economic systems must be understood and assessed across three dimensions: the individual, the society, and the species. First, it is necessary to consider the impact of a decision on the individual person directly affected by the situation. Second, the effects on society must be considered, including how policies or decisions impact local communities, governments, and cultural norms. Finally, decisions must be examined for their broader effects on the human species and global ecosystem. This wider perspective considers how actions in one society or region can ripple outward influencing the global community and planet for generations.

Balancing these three dimensions is key to making decisions that are both morally sound and practical. In some cases, decisions may benefit one dimension more than another, such as when a policy improves society as a whole but causes temporary discomfort for the individual. These trade-offs must be carefully considered, ensuring that the benefits outweigh the harms in the long term. The goal is to create solutions that maximize equity and minimize exploitation, while also acknowledging the complexities of each dimension.

In conclusion, equity leadership and objective morality offer a comprehensive approach to addressing the challenges faced by our modern society. We live in a tumultuous age with challenges that threaten both our daily lives and the longevity of the species. At no other time in human history have we faced these herculean problems. At no other time in the history of the United States has this country needed to live up to its mythology more than now. This framework, and the forthcoming ideas and suggestions, are curated to build a society that reflects the ideals of liberty, equity and morality. Together we can overcome this torrent of darkness and rise into a utopia with principled leaders and prosperity for all.

What If I Just Don't Care

In the lead-up to every election, TV commercials, debates, social media discussions, and political campaigns saturate the public sphere. After the ballots are cast, many people feel exhausted and likely disappointed, so they retreat into apathy. The fact is there is little reason to care because for 50 years we have not had leaders who actually want to solve problems. They want to perpetuate hope and fear because that gets them elected. If they solve problems, what would they run on? Even still, a significant part of American culture is politics. Many of us strongly identify ourselves by our political views. Yet many millions of eligible voters do not vote. We know them, they are our neighbors and friends. These individuals often avoid political conversations, perhaps adhering to the old: "never discuss money, politics, or religion."

For these people, apathy or disengagement is their chosen response.

If you are one of these people, I kindly request you remove your head from that moist dark hole. I respect your intention, but it is no longer an option. Nostalgic apathy will lead us all to a doomscape. As citizens, we have a responsibility to shape our nation. This does not mean that everyone needs to be deeply involved in politics or constantly debating issues, but it does require an understanding of one's place in a democracy. Elections affect everyone's lives, and the decisions you make impact not just on the present but future generations as well. For example, there are decisions made during the Reagan administration, especially regarding economic and judicial policies, that still affect the nation today[ii]. While it may seem easier to ignore politics, in this age of immoral Trumpism doing so is a dereliction of your life.

If you choose apathy, you're relinquishing control over your life, convincing yourself that government doesn't matter. But the truth is that the government affects your life in profound ways. Your paycheck, the cleanliness of your food and water, and countless other aspects of your daily existence are directly influenced by the policies of elected officials. From local politicians to national leaders, every election matters. The choices you make are real.

It's understandable to feel exhausted by the complexity

and negativity of politics. But instead of retreating into indifference, take ownership of your life and your choices. If no political figure resonates with you or your values, seek out others who share your perspective. Better yet, run for office yourself. Engage in conversations, discuss what you don't like about certain candidates or policies, and find like-minded individuals. You may discover that someone close to you feels the same way, and that could spark the beginning of real change. Ultimately, if the candidates don't perfectly align with your beliefs, vote for the one who comes closest, even if you disagree with them on certain issues or if you just do not "like" them. Voting for someone who aligns somewhat with your views is better than abstaining altogether.

At the end of the day, your voice matters as much as anyone else's. Choosing not to vote, ignoring the system, or staying silent is the path to tyranny. It's silence that allows harmful policies and broken systems to persist unchecked. You live in a country where your perspective is vital for everyone's well-being. Throughout history, some citizens have squandered their power indirectly costing millions of people their lives through war, conflict, and bad policies.

Stop the cycle, get involved.

Government Shmoverment: Who needs it?

In the United States, we debate on the extent of the government all the time. One side advocates for a larger government, usually aligned with liberal ideology, while the other supports a smaller government, which aligns with conservative views. But these discussions never touch on what value government actually has.

Government can be viewed as:

- A bureaucracy that is amorphous, endless and powerful yet inept

or

- An entity that has a unique capacity to more effectively address challenges than to other kinds of organizations.

The first view is a consequence of apathetic leadership that has allowed systemic decline in government services for political purposes. We can solve that with better leaders. The second view highlights why attempts to improve government efficiency through privatization or severe funding cuts are fundamentally flawed and destined to fail.

The fundamental difference between the private sector and the government lies in scaled power. Most corporations must respond to market forces. If they fail to adjust their offerings, they lose out. However, governments and monopolies are the exception. Monopolies are not subject to market forces because they have no competition, allowing them to force consumers into whatever offer the monopoly wants. However, a monopoly is still beholden to owners which means it concentrates unchecked power in the hands of a few, leaving consumers almost powerless.

Ultimately, the government functions in a somewhat similar way. Governments possess unique power to compel compliance and provide services that no private entity can offer on the same scale. People may criticize or even hate the government, but they still rely on it for essential services, such as identification, security and boring things like building and health standards, unemployment insurance, and a safe investment. Government is the power people have against monopolies.

History proves this concept in that revolutionaries seeking to overthrow a government fight to replace the institution rather than destroy it. In this sense, the government's brand is raw, universally recognized power. Governments, unlike corporations, have the capacity to impel and empower citizens with a level of authority no corporation can match.

Corporations are essentially dictatorships led by an owner or a board which wields ultimate authority over its employees and consumers. In contrast, the U.S. government is a federalist republican democracy designed to distribute power among individuals. While not all people have equal access to power, everyone receives some level of service and representation from the government. The government doesn't exist to turn a profit, and its officials don't receive ownership stakes in the country. Thus, they are theoretically incentivized to work on behalf of the people and not themselves. If the politician wants to keep their job and status, they must work for the voters.

Undeniably it would be naïve to think that corruption and graft are not integral to the government paradigm, but corruption is also the point. The government can provide services at cost, or even at a loss. Most corporations cannot afford to do so, which is why corruption exists. After all, if a corporate structure could achieve equal power to the government, why buy politicians?

Governments, unlike private entities, operate without the pressure of profit, allowing them to prioritize the needs of all citizens, especially the most vulnerable such as children, the elderly, and the poor. In a capitalist society, privatizing public services in healthcare, food, and shelter assistance will inevitably exclude some people. The fact is that corporations are designed to focus on profit not outcomes. Meanwhile, nonprofits are designed to be narrowly targeted. So, the only type of organization that can morally and equitably provide for the welfare of all people, address macroscale problems, and give security and assurance is the government.

At the end of the day, the government fills the gaps where the market fails. History shows that societies cannot thrive without government oversight and intervention, making its role essential in meeting the basic needs of all humans. Even still, every day we can read about or experience some aspects of government that are painful, overcomplicated, or deeply flawed. Change and improvement in the system is absolutely needed. Government, like all organizations, must innovate and evolve. But innovation does not require destruction. Bureaucracy is not the enemy of efficiency. The only problem with government is that our leaders have become so apathetic and comfortable in the status quo that they are seeking continuing resolutions rather than solutions. If you want a government that works better, get leaders who understand what makes a government powerful while being willing to actually address issues with creativity and innovation. After all, size does not really matter, it is all about how you use it.

Why Democracy Tho'?

It is wonderful to discuss a vision for a prosperous society and a principled republic but as voters we do not make decisions based on the morality of the politics. We care about what impacts our daily lives. So, what does a principled republic do for you? We'll discuss the answer to that question later. But I contend, there is a more fundamental question in this age of rising authoritarianism: What is so good about democracy anyway?

Democracy ensures that individuals have a say in who governs them, which in turn provides them with agency over their lives. Under authoritarian regimes, the needs of the common people are often overlooked in favor of those in power. Since the common people have nothing to do with keeping that leader in wealth and power, there is no incentive for the leader to be beholden to the people. Democracy, by contrast, ensures that the voices of many are heard, and decisions are made collectively, ideally in a way that meets the needs of the majority.

For society, democracy is valuable because it ensures equity survives for the long term. The relative equity of a society is measured by how well it balances individual needs with collective needs[iii]. If one person's desires negatively affect the greater good, democracy provides mechanisms to correct this imbalance. This is what makes democracy essential for society's function. The democratic process is a kind of immune system for the worst impulses of humans. If enough people vote, the wisdom of the crowd will always ensure incremental progress towards a more equitable future. Nonetheless, it requires active participation. Purposeful action is what makes the difference between the splendid gardens of a regal palace and the dying plant in your living room . It is also what keeps democracy from being overrun with fascism.

When it comes to the species, democracy holds value because it allows both individuals and society to find equity within a larger, interconnected system. Civilization, made up of individuals and societies, thrives when all parties can achieve equity and prosperity. Thus, when individuals and societies experience fairness and agency within a democracy, civilization as a whole can reflect that progress and build from it.

At the end of the day, democracy is the best of the imperfect ways to govern ourselves. It provides agency for the individual, stability for society, and is our best shot for achieving equity for the species. The whims of powerful authoritarians and the natural instability that these kinds of regimes are why humanity has never achieved world peace. The fact is that democracy is still an infantile system in the course of history. Time and effort from you, me and everyone else will help the system to improve. The magic is that the fundamental structure of democracy gives little old you the key to achieving progress.

Equitable Leadership

In American mythology, there's a widely held belief that anyone can succeed here; it's the land of opportunity. This idea holds that anyone who works hard and has determination can achieve greatness, regardless of their starting point. While there is truth in this, there is also a pervasive myth that undermines it. For many people, hard work alone isn't enough to reach the top because genuine wealth is extremely rare. This is a consequence of capitalism. In a capitalist society, there are only so many positions of power and so much wealth to go around. As a result, there will always be some people who end up doing the "dirty work" and receiving lower wages, while others become disproportionately wealthy.

That said, prosperity is a relative term. In capitalism,

there doesn't need to be widespread poverty, but there will always be poorer people relative to the wealthy. Whether in capitalist or communist systems, human societies have always had a dynamic where there are those with power and those without. This power disparity creates a hierarchy in society. The American myth suggests that wealth creates power but the truth is more complex than just having money.

In America, political power is a reflection of other forms of power— social status, racial privilege, cultural influence, and wealth. Today, the loudest voices, often from a minority, dominate political discourse. In the age of social media, the adage that "the squeaky wheel gets the grease" is truer than ever, with a vocal minority often steering the conversation. This creates a silenced majority—the people whose voices are not heard amid the noise of the powerful.

A government that truly supports equity must acknowledge these silenced groups. Leaders should understand that the loud and powerful are just one perspective. For a leader to focus solely on this minority is a disgrace to the majority of constituents. The leader must make decisions based on what's best for everyone, including those whose voices are not often heard.

So how does a leader know what is equitable when they're hearing only from the powerful? This is where the 21st century offers a unique opportunity. Technology and data allow leaders to break through the noise. They can survey, poll, analyze studies, and use social media to gather feedback. The silenced majority may not be loud, but they are still there, and it's possible to hear them if you listen closely. A leader should look beyond the narratives and solutions presented by the powerful and seek alternatives. They can use data, social media, and expert opinions to explore other perspectives. Even better, leaders can connect with the people in their own communities, their families, neighbors, and everyday citizens, to better understand the needs and desires of the broader population.

The worst leaders are those who assume they already know what's best, and the second worst are those who only listen to the powerful. True leaders are those who stand for equity, making decisions that truly serve the needs of all people. This is the America that can live up to its mythology—the land of opportunity for everyone, not just the powerful few.

On Liberty and Its Responsibility

At the core of the American ideology lies the belief that individuals are capable of making decisions for themselves, better than any divine king or authoritarian could dictate. This principle emerged in the 18th century, at a time when most nations were still ruled by monarchs who claimed their power by divine right. But then came a group of English colonists who, feeling oppressed by British Parliament and the King, sought independence. At that time, there was no established king or structure to take his place in the colonies. These men didn't claim divine authority, nor did they want to create a monarchy. Instead, they operated within a federalist system, governed by multiple bodies and councils, which allowed for the participation of the people in decision-making[iv].

The birth of the United States was founded on the assumption that people have the power to govern themselves, and liberty became the currency of this assumption. Liberty, in this sense, is the freedom to make choices about the circumstances and structures of one's life, and the freedom to assess and define how well the government serves the people. In the Declaration of Independence, Thomas Jefferson wrote "But when a long train of abuses and usurpations, pursuing invariably the same Object evinces a design to reduce them under absolute Despotism, it is their right, it is their duty, to throw off such Government, and to provide new Guards for their future security[v]." In other words, it is the duty of the people to rise up and change the government if it ceases to serve them effectively. The fundamental liberty that Americans hold—and by extension, other democracies around the world—is the idea that there is no king or divine intervention that determines who governs. The people have the power to decide and to change.

Liberty does not mean the freedom to do absolutely anything without consequences. It's important to recognize that while we are free to think whatever we want, there are social and legal rules that govern our actions. The rules are not meant to stifle individual expression; they're about creating peace and harmony within society. As social creatures, humans operate in a context that ensures our survival and our ability to reproduce. On a human level, if we create chaos, division, or violence, we effectively undermine our ability to live fulfilling lives and ensure the continuation of our species. That's why there are things we cannot say or do in public, not because our freedom is restricted, but because we must consider the effects on others and on the society.

The actions of an individual accumulate across groups to form the fabric of social behavior. The rules of society are extension of this process at full scale. These social rules are not arbitrary; they are designed to protect us and maintain the fabric of society. If you decide not to be a force of destruction or division in your community, you contribute to the social order, which increases your chances of living a fulfilling and prosperous life.

Here's the kicker, you have the liberty to make that decision. We have the freedom to express ourselves, but with that comes the responsibility to consider the consequences of our words and actions in the larger social context. The reality is that there are no rules. There are only decisions and consequences. If you decide you want to live in a society of compassion, you can create one. If you decide to live in a society of hate, you can create one too. Your actions are your freedoms. With actions comes consequences. Hate and violence give license for hate and violence such that no one is immune to it. Thus, if you want to live peacefully, you must take actions that create peace. That is the power, the promise, and the burden of liberty.

In countries without such liberties, the people do not have a choice in those decisions. For example, in Iran, during certain periods of its history, the Islamic clerics dictated the rules of society, from what books could be read to how daily rituals were performed. These were not merely social customs; they were laws based on divine interpretation, and the idea of a constitutional government was considered heretical by religious authorities. It wasn't until the late 19th century that Iranians gained access to the same philosophical texts that inspired the creation of the American Constitution. Even then, the idea of establishing a constitutional system within the context of their Islamic philosophy proved to be incredibly difficult. Thus, whether one followed and believe the religious beliefs of the clerics or not, they were forced to live by those precepts or face death or exile[vi]. Similar circumstances have occurred in Russian and China and other areas around the world at different points in history whenever a powerful class makes choices for everyone. The critical lesson is that choice still exists in those place, but the choice is between compliance or death. In the US and other countries that value liberty, the choices and consequences are much more nuanced.

This comparison underscores the uniqueness of the liberty we enjoy in the United States, where we are free to think and express ourselves and make decisions that impact our lives. This liberty, however, requires a delicate balance. A government that supports liberty must allow individuals to have power over their own lives but also provide guardrails to ensure that society, as a whole, remains harmonious. For instance, while individuals have the right to defend themselves, the government establishes laws that define the circumstances under which force is justified—such as in self-defense.

This balance is at the heart of American governance. The purpose of laws and regulations is not to limit freedom, but to ensure that everyone's liberty is protected. This means that one person's freedom should not infringe upon another's. The government's role is to maintain this balance, ensuring that society functions in a way that allows each individual the opportunity to thrive without disrupting the lives of others.

In some situations, individuals may feel constrained by the law, especially if they strongly desire something that is prohibited. But these laws exist to prevent harm and maintain the common good. Unfortunately, individuals may still break the law, and when they do, society must enact the consequences for those actions just as a parent may discipline a child. Ultimately, the goal of any government that upholds liberty is to ensure that all citizens have the opportunity to live freely, responsibly, and harmoniously, contributing to the well-being of the larger community.

On Morality and When Government Should STFU

In American politics, there is a common tendency to use moral arguments to justify policy stances. This approach can be seen in the arguments made by Democrats against Donald Trump in the 2020 and 2024 elections, and in the pro-life stance adopted by Republicans and conservatives, along with their focus on "family values." However, all these definitions of morality are fluid and inconsistent.

For instance, the pro-life movement argues that abortion is immoral because it involves ending a life, and life, according to their perspective, begins at conception. While the claim may seem moral on the surface, it ignores the dignity and rights of the woman who is carrying the child. A truly moral cause cannot sacrifice the well-being of one individual to support another.

When it comes to abortion, the government's role should be centered on what preserves liberty and equity. In the American ethos, this requires an emphasis on individual liberty and a policy that can be universally applied regardless of specific medical circumstance. This equitable approach is the most moral because it does not rank the lives of one person over another. Thus, the only position on abortion that an American government should take is that the choice should lie with the woman herself; whether she decides to keep the baby, possibly even against medical advice, or whether she decides that abortion is the best option for her life and circumstances. The idea that third-trimester abortions would be used frivolously is unlikely, as rational, mentally healthy individuals do not choose to abort late in pregnancy without serious reasons. Moreover, doctors are bound by a moral code that prioritizes the life and safety of the mother, and in situations where the baby is not viable or the mother's life is at risk, a late-term abortion might be medically necessary.[vii]

Morality, in this context, is about making decisions that prioritize the individual's needs, especially those who are weak, vulnerable, or less powerful. The question may be asked: isn't the fetus weak, vulnerable, and less powerful? Absolutely but this means that the decision needs to prioritize what is best for that particular fetus at that point in time. Government, by its very nature, must operate under rules that apply universally. This creates challenges in situations that involve complex moral decisions, such as abortion. In these cases, the government's broad policies often cannot account for the nuanced individual circumstances that make each case unique. When these complexities arise, it is the government's responsibility to step back and allow individuals to make those decisions for themselves to execute their liberty. It is essential that leaders ask whether government policies uphold morality and whether they respect the rights and autonomy of the individual. Policies that harm, disadvantage, or discriminate against individuals or groups are morally wrong and should be opposed. A government that seeks to avoid harming its citizens, especially its most vulnerable, is a government that is morally sound.

In the broader context of American society, there is a danger in adopting a moral framework that justifies harm in the name of the "greater good." This type of moral reasoning can enable policies that discriminate against individuals, especially when they are viewed as exceptions to the norm. The government, therefore, must be held to a higher standard of individual rights and protection.

While individual moral beliefs may vary widely, it is critical that the government upholds a universal moral principle that protects each individual's dignity. As citizens and voters, we must ensure that our leaders reflect this commitment to individual rights and fairness. To do otherwise would be to support policies that are morally flawed and detrimental to the health of society as a whole.

If we examine the history of the United States and its policies, we must recognize that many past policies have been morally indefensible. It is not enough to overlook or ignore these mistakes; we must confront them head-on, recognizing that a healthy society must hold individual morality at its core. In doing so, we affirm our commitment to a government that values and protects the lives and rights of all its citizens.

America is Multicultural; sry, not sry

For years now, the United States has been engulfed in what politicians and the media call a "culture war." At its core, this "war" pits various groups against one another: those who believe American culture should be defined by white, Christian, traditionalist values, those who reject that notion entirely, and a broad spectrum of people somewhere in between. But the reality is far simpler.

From its inception as British and French colonies over 400 years ago, the United States has always been multicultural. There has never been a time when this land was not a mosaic of diverse peoples and perspectives. For centuries, compromises among these differing groups have been the cornerstone of building anything resembling a cohesive society. However, the balance of power has heavily favored those of European ancestry, resulting in persistent issues of discrimination and racial inequality. Yet, these challenges aren't the entirety of American culture—they are distortions within it.[viii]

American culture, at its heart, is not singular. Instead, it is an extraordinary collection of microcultures. Every culture in the world is represented here in some form, blending and evolving in unique ways. Interestingly, there are arguably only two distinctly American cultures: the Western cowboy ethos and Black culture. Both were born from the specific conditions of the United States, yet they, too, are diverse and complex. Black culture, in particular, has been profoundly influential, permeating every ethnic group and even extending beyond U.S. borders. This cultural sharing exemplifies the deeply multicultural nature of American society and humanity in general. This should be a point of immense pride for our nation.

The so-called culture war, then, is a conflict between those who value diversity as an intrinsic part of America's identity and those who resist it. Some cling to a notion of ethnic or moral superiority rooted in white, Christian, traditionalist ideals, viewing these as society's bedrock. Importantly, no one aspect or achievement of human civilization can be attributed to a single race. The Aryan supposition that white culture has an outsized history is not factual nor coherent. Meanwhile, imposing one cultural framework on a nation as diverse as the United States is an inherently futile and destructive effort—a square peg in a round hole.

In the modern era, identity politics has risen to prominence. Concepts like gender, sexuality, and identity are being explored and understood in ways that challenge long-held norms. This evolution unsettles some, who fear it threatens the reality they once knew. But this cultural shift is not just inevitable; it is natural. Society evolves, just as it has with issues like monotheistic religion, interracial marriage or women's rights—issues that were once taboo but are now broadly accepted, though challenges remain.

For those who find these changes disconcerting, it's worth recognizing that this discomfort stems from encountering something new, not something inherently wrong. Cultural evolution is unsettling precisely because it pushes us to rethink our assumptions. Yet, just as society has adapted to previous cultural shifts, we will adapt to these as well. Remember, the inception of the Jewish religion in Egypt was a significant cultural shift as was the arrival of Jesus in those lands. Cultural evolution is a fact of human civilization.

For those embracing these new paradigms, it's vital to understand that being a trailblazer is challenging, but it's part of creating a broader, more inclusive culture. It is more vital than ever that as a trailblazer you exercise compassion for those who have yet to join with your view. People who do not understand your perspective or feel threatened by it are not automatically evil people – perhaps they have a deep seeded bigotry or most likely, they don't understand and are reacting with anxiety and fear. Either way, as Thomas Paine said, "time will make more converts than reason."[ix] Stay strong but stay compassionate. And to those on the other side, you are not required to understand. Simply having respect and compassion towards those who are different is healthier, more constructive, and more sustainable than hate and fear.

Identity politics is not a sign of division; it's a mechanism for greater self-awareness. Politics has always intersected with identity—policies and decisions have always affected different groups in different ways. The goal should be to create solutions that uphold liberty, equity, and morality for everyone, recognizing that this requires compromise and mutual understanding. Only by embracing our differences and learning from them can we progress as a society.

If, however, someone finds it intolerable to live among diverse perspectives, then the United States may not be the right place for them. This country was built on the foundation of diversity, and its strength lies in its ability to accommodate and celebrate differences. There are other places in the world where monocultural values dominate, and perhaps such individuals would feel more at home there. But I would also encourage self-reflection. The world is becoming more interconnected and less accommodating of insular thinking. As the global population grows and land, water and other resources becomes scarcer, tolerance will not just be ideal; it will be a necessity.

America has a unique opportunity to lead by example, embodying the future of humanity, a future built on respect, tolerance, and the dignity of every individual. If America can live up to its ideals, it will show the world how to navigate the complexities of a diverse and interdependent planet. This is the challenge and the promise of our time.

On Race in America

Race is not a biological fact, but rather a social and political construct. Historian Jim Horton emphasizes this important point, noting that race is a concept created and perpetuated by society.[x] In the context of the United States, it is clear that race has been used to justify a pervasive and systemic form of discrimination. This reality must be acknowledged in any honest assessment of the nation's past.

However, civil discourse around race is crucial. It must be maintained and highlighted at all levels of society. Multiculturalism and racial integration are significant advantages, both economically and politically, for the country and for every community within it. It is the moral responsibility of the government to address and mitigate statistical racial disparities, though racism itself cannot be legislated out of existence. Instead, it must be confronted on an individual level, with people choosing to appreciate the individuality of each person and recognizing the important role racial identity plays in shaping a person's sense of self.

While it is reprehensible for anyone to act on racist impulses, it must be understood that race will continue to be a factor in how people identify and navigate the world. People will inevitably make distinctions based on race, but society must decide that it is acceptable for individuals to identify with their racial background and live their lives through that lens—historically, morally, culturally, and ethnically. Discrimination, harassment, and judgment have no place in a society that values liberty, equity, and morality.

America's power lies in its multiculturalism, tolerance, and the strength found in diverse perspectives and histories. At the same time, we must recognize that our history is one of oppression, mistakes, and bad ideas that have shaped structures within society. We can never fully undo the damage caused by these past actions; there is no amount of financial reparations or equity that can make up for the centuries of injustice without fundamentally disrupting modern society. That said, we must begin to treat the many cultures, peoples, and identities that make up our society with the dignity, respect, and the sovereignty they deserve — rights that should have been afforded to them by previous generations.

Racism will not simply disappear. But as a society we can work to fix the systems and structures that make it a disadvantage to belong to a certain racial group. As individuals, we can adopt a more compassionate approach to dealing with our racial insecurities and desires. No one race should be privileged over another in any aspect of society. Yet, we must acknowledge that we live in a society where this remains the reality. No race should bear the shame of the actions of their ancestors, but we must also learn to forgive ourselves and move past our own prejudices. Only through forgiveness, acknowledgment, and an understanding of where these ideas originated can we begin to develop a healthier relationship with race.

This shift will take time. No government or politician can promise to eliminate racism or solve the "race problem." There is no singular "race problem." What exists are statistical disparities, historical injustices, and present-day repercussions that we must work to address. Once we begin addressing these issues and building a culture that appreciates diversity and difference—one that finds strength in our shared humanity and differing perspectives—only then will we achieve the true vision of America that we believe in.

On Shutting Up about Free Speech

One of America's most frequent political arguments revolves around free speech. People often claim that their free speech rights are being violated by various actions, especially when they face consequences like being blocked or banned on social media. However, there's an important concept about free speech that is frequently overlooked. This misunderstanding fuels division and discomfort, especially among politicians who struggle to address these concerns.

The First Amendment of the U.S. Constitution states, "Congress shall make no law... abridging the freedom of speech...," therein lies the limits of free speech.[xi] This means that the government, at all levels, cannot create laws that restrict or punish free speech. A notable example comes from a Supreme Court case called Schenck v US from 1919, where a young person distributed anti-draft leaflets and was charged under the Espionage act. The defendant argued that the leaflets were free speech and thus the government was illegally suppressing their rights by charging them with a crime. The Supreme Court upheld that the leaflets represented a "clear and present danger" and thus were not protected under the first amendment. The key is that free speech does not mean that you can say anything you want, it means you can speak the truth to government, but you cannot cause danger with your words. If your words create harm, the government does have to power and responsibility to silence you (RE: Alex Jones). There is a fine line, however, between speech that harms and speech that offends. If a person uses racial slurs but does not threaten violence, the law may allow that speech. However, if the speech is accompanied by a threat, such as saying, "I'm going to kill you, you [insert racial slur]" that would cross the line into illegal territory. As a culture, we have a lot of work to figure out how to communicate and address generational traumas that show up in language. But that work is not the job of the government—it is on us, as individuals, to figure out within ourselves and among our community. The government's role is to ensure justice when someone gets hurt in the process.

All that being said, what about a corporation? Can a movie theater make a policy that says if you yell "fire" in their theater erroneously, they have the right to ban you from attending again? Yes, private companies can set their own rules. The first amendment restrict only applies to the government-- everyone else can restrict speech however they want. Social media platforms can ban, or censor content based on their policies. If you disagree with a platform's moderation policies, the solution is simple: don't use that platform. This is the principle of free market economics—if you don't like a company's policies, you are free to choose another one.

In contrast to countries like Russia, where people can be arrested for expressing political opinions or carrying certain flags, the United States prides itself on the freedom to express diverse viewpoints. People can wear whatever flags they want, even those associated with controversial or extremist ideologies. However, they must also be prepared for the consequences of expressing such views. If someone waves a fascist flag, for example, they should expect opposition, just as someone who supports anti-fascist views might face opposition from those who disagree with them. This back-and-forth is not a threat to democracy; it's the heart of free speech. Both sides—fascists and anti-fascists—must be able to engage in non-violent dialogue.

The purpose of free speech, as enshrined in the First Amendment, is to create a space for open discussion and debate, allowing society to examine different ideas and decide what kind of nation it wants to be. Through this discourse, we have the power to shape the future of our country. If a majority of people support a particular ideology, that's the direction the country will take, for better or worse. But the key is that this process happens through discussion, through debate, and through the votes we cast.

This ability to change and evolve as a society is what makes the U.S. system so powerful. We have an immune system for our country—an ability to identify harmful ideas and, if necessary, correct them without violence. This immune system works because we are allowed to speak freely, to challenge ideas, and to decide, as a society, what values we want to embrace. Speech is the vehicle through which we hold our democracy accountable and ensure that our nation reflects the beliefs and values of its people.

When States' Rights are Right and Wrong

In conservative circles, the concept of "states' rights" is frequently touted as a foundational principle of governance. However, this idea has a fraught history, one that dates back to its pivotal role in creating the Civil War. The conflict arose from a division between states that supported slavery and those that opposed it. At its core, the war stemmed from disagreements over whether new states should be allowed to determine their stance on slavery or if the federal government should step in to ensure a national standard. The South's insistence on state sovereignty clashed with the two concurrent movements. First was the federalist perspective that wanted the federal government to regulate where slavery would be allowed in the US so as to ensure equity. Secondly, there was a strong abolitionist movement that advocated that there was a moral and political imperative to curtail slavery. Thus, the country was fractured between abolitionists, people who were not opposed to slavery but were not economically dependent on it, and those who were economically dependent on it. There was also a very popular bigotry and dehumanization towards black people that fueled the policy debate in the first place. These competing factions revealed the fundamental tension between individual state autonomy and the federal government's role in shaping national ethics and equity.

This debate over states' rights did not end with the Civil War. It resurfaced in modern issues, such as abortion rights. For decades, conservatives have argued against federally guaranteed abortion access, claiming that states should have the power to legislate this issue independently. This perspective reflects a broader interpretation of America's founding: the belief that the United States originated as 13 independent colonies that chose to collaborate while retaining their individual sovereignty. However, this narrative has significant flaws.

First, the colonies united against Britain because they shared common grievances under British rule. The British Crown viewed them collectively, and only by banding together could the colonies hope to achieve independence. No single colony could have stood alone against the might of the British Empire.[iv] This lesson underscores the importance of national unity over individual autonomy when facing shared challenges.

Second, the idea of state sovereignty as a standalone principle ignores the practical reality that many states depend on federal resources to function. Poorer states, particularly in the South, rely heavily on federal funding generated by taxes from wealthier states like California and New York.[xiv] This interconnected economic system demonstrates that the United States operates as an ecosystem, where the strength of one part supports the whole.

The three levels of government—federal, state, and local—exist to balance this ecosystem. Each level addresses issues appropriate to its scope. Just as a corporation relies on a structured hierarchy, with middle management handling regional concerns and executives focusing on overarching strategies, governance requires a similar structure. State governments, like middle managers, have the autonomy to address specific, localized issues. However, they cannot wield more power than the federal government, just as middle managers cannot override corporate executives.

Certain issues transcend local or state boundaries and demand federal oversight. Matters like access to healthcare or judicial reform, which affect individuals in every corner of the nation, require federal intervention. For example, abortion laws, since the overturning of Roe v. Wade, have varied widely among states, forcing individuals to cross state lines to access healthcare. This patchwork approach undermines national cohesion and creates inequities. Issues of such universal importance require a federal framework to ensure consistency, fairness, and moral accountability.

Allowing states to decide such issues independently risks creating inconsistencies that undermine the nation's moral, legal, and social fabric. The federal government must maintain a "thumb on the scale" to uphold liberty, equity, and morality for all citizens, regardless of their state of residence; this is why millions of Americans died in the Civil War in the name of the Union. If we let that function of the federal government to be undermined, then the Civil War was fought in vain.

Conversely, some matters are better left to states. Localized issues, such as managing Texas's unique energy grid or tailoring labor regulations for workers in different climates, are well-suited for state governance. States should have the flexibility to enact policies that address their specific circumstances, whether it's regulating hunting laws to maintain ecological balance or adapting housing and education policies to specific population demographics. These are the types of decisions where states' rights make sense and where federal interference may be counterproductive.

Ultimately, our leaders must strike a balance. States' rights have their place, particularly in addressing localized concerns. But when issues have national implications or touch on fundamental rights, the Federal government must ensure a cohesive, fair, and just society. Recognizing this distinction is crucial to navigating the complex relationship between state and federal authority in a way that strengthens the nation as a whole. Failure to do so is demonstrably dangerous.

The Pragmatism of Separating Church and State

The First Amendment of the United States Constitution explicitly states that "Congress shall make no law respecting an establishment of religion or prohibiting the free exercise thereof..."[xi] This was a key point of the founding vision for the United States. From its earliest days, the country was designed with a secular structure, largely influenced by figures such as Benjamin Franklin, who was essentially an atheist, and Thomas Jefferson, who was a devout Christian.[iv] This diversity in belief systems reflected a broader, multicultural society that was integral to the country's creation. The Founding Fathers, recognizing the complexity of a nation that was made up of various religious and cultural groups, saw the necessity of keeping government and religion separate.

This separation was not just a practical consideration; it was also about creating a framework where all people, regardless of religion, could coexist peacefully. At the time, the colonies were made up of people from different backgrounds—some were Christians, some were Jews, others followed indigenous beliefs, and many were enslaved Africans with their own religious practices. The United States needed a government structure that could unite some of these groups under one banner without privileging any single belief system.

One of the crucial reasons for this separation of church and state was to avoid the inherent danger of disenfranchising any one group. Historically, when a government establishes a state religion, it automatically excludes those who do not adhere to that religion. This exclusion can lead to discontent and, eventually, to unrest, because people naturally resist being oppressed. [vi] The Founding Fathers seem to have understood this dynamic and sought to create a system that would prevent any group from being marginalized based on their religious beliefs.

Moreover, the American experiment was built on the idea that people can govern themselves without the need for a divine right to rule. This was a radical departure from systems of government where rulers claimed their authority from a higher power. The establishment of the United States as a democracy meant rejecting the idea of kings or God-given rulers. A separation between church and state was essential to maintain this concept. Without it, there would be the risk of theocracy or religious dictatorship, which would undermine the democratic foundation of the country.

However, the separation of church and state does not mean that individual politicians or leaders must abandon their religious beliefs. Everyone is free to express their faith and incorporate it into their personal lives. That said, when making policy decisions, especially those that affect a diverse population, leaders must ensure that their religious beliefs do not dictate their political actions. A politician's moral or ethical stance must be grounded in universal principles that apply to all citizens, not just those who share their religious views. If a policy based on religious beliefs results in the oppression of others, it runs counter to the American ideal of liberty, equity, and justice.

The question that must be asked, especially when making laws, is whether the policy is inclusive or whether it inadvertently marginalizes certain groups. For example, setting policies that align only with Christian values can disenfranchise non-Christian citizens. Christian values may align with American ideals if those values are broad and universal enough to support the principles of justice and equality for all.

The key point is that the government should not use religion as the basis for policy decisions. This does not diminish the importance of religion in individuals' lives, but it ensures that laws are crafted in a way that respects the diversity of beliefs in the country. If an individual wants to follow a strict religious code, there are nations where such systems exist—such as Afghanistan, Israel, or Iran—but these systems often lead to instability and disenfranchisement. The United States, by contrast, was designed to be a society where individuals have the freedom to follow their own beliefs without government interference.

Therefore, maintaining a separation of church and state is crucial for the longevity and health of the nation. It prevents any one group from imposing their beliefs on others, ensuring that all citizens can live in a society that respects their right to believe as they choose. This principle is at the heart of the American experiment and must be upheld to preserve the vision of the Founding Fathers—a vision of a nation built on freedom, justice, and inclusivity.

Data and the Final Frontier

The rapid pace of technological change is one of the most significant factors disrupting political structures worldwide, including in the United States. This phenomenon is not new; throughout history, technological advancements have outpaced societal evolution, leading to profound shifts in the way societies operate. Ray Kurzweil, a futurist, has written extensively about this accelerating pace of technological progress, a pattern identified by many other thinkers as well.[xv] Technology advances exponentially, and these developments trigger societal changes.

For instance, the mechanization of the 19th century opened up new opportunities for urban living, shifting the economy away from agrarian, farm-based systems to mechanized manufacturing. Similarly, the shift from mechanization to computerization in the 20th century transitioned economies from manufacturing to service-based industries, which continues today. Each of these technological shifts reshapes the fabric of society.

The printing press, which revolutionized the spread of information, catalyzed the Protestant Reformation and altered the religious and political landscape of Europe. In a similar way, the advent of the internet and social media has transformed politics, particularly by changing how information is disseminated and how people engage in political discourse.[xvi] We are now at a point where traditional political strategies no longer function effectively. The methods that dominated the 20th century, like newspaper campaigns and kissing babies, have been upended by new forms of communication, such as social media.

The crucial takeaway here is understanding the relationship between technology and society. Any rational, functional government must recognize that advances in science and technology can have a profound impact on the quality of people's lives and the overall structure of society. This makes government regulation of science and technology absolutely essential.

Governments often fail to react quickly enough to these changes, as they tend to operate from a reactive, rather than proactive, stance. When major technological shifts occur, they must be anticipated, and governments must act swiftly. A data-driven government that values science and trusts experts is crucial in this context. Having experts in key areas ensures that leadership can respond rapidly to technological shifts, preventing harm to individuals and society. In some cases, governments can even leverage these advancements to benefit society, as seen in Estonia.

Estonia, a former poor, corrupt soviet state, embraced the internet early on in the 1990s. Today, it boasts the most digitized government in the world, offering 99% of government services online. Citizens can pay taxes in minutes and even vote from anywhere in the world. This demonstrates the power of technology to solve complex problems. Technology can improve processes across the board, offering solutions that are more efficient, secure, and cost-effective than current systems.[xvii]

For example, issues like voter fraud, entitlement applications, and ensuring citizens receive needed services could be addressed through technology and data-driven governance. A society founded by a renowned scientist, Benjamin Franklin, should value science because it can improve the quality of life for its citizens and ensure a functional, prosperous nation.

While some may fear science contradicts their religious beliefs, good leadership can quell these anxieties. First of all, the purpose of science in this technological context is not about defining beginnings, meanings or reality but about providing tangible benefits like improved healthcare, better infrastructure, and more efficient economies. Science is the singular proven method humanity has to improve the quality of life. Religious beliefs and science will clash but that is a conflict between yourself and your beliefs that must be addressed on an individual level. Again, our moral imperative as a society is to ensure that government is separate from religious influence. Thus, we must embrace science to solve universal issues.

One of the most pressing issues today, climate change, exemplifies the importance of science in policy making. Regardless of its origins, climate change is real. There is no denying the real world changes we see around the world every day. If we accept that something is different with our climate than it was 10,20, 50 or 100+ years ago (all of which are backed by data), then policies based on scientific data are the only way to effectively address it. This reality is born from 500 years of human experience. The alternative is inaction or prayer. Prayer may be necessary too but why not use every tool at our disposable to increase the long-term prospects of humanity.

Furthermore, embracing science allows for progress in key areas such as space exploration. Many question the value of space exploration, but it is essential for a number of reasons. The growing human population demands new resources to support global prosperity. Earth is a finite resource, and space exploration provides a pathway to acquire new resources and technologies. If humanity can figure out how to live on the moon or Mars, it will unlock the solutions needed to address poverty and resource scarcity on Earth. The technological advancements required for space colonization will have far-reaching benefits, improving life in a myriad of ways. This is why investing in space exploration is crucial — it's not just about discovering new frontiers but also about advancing technology for the betterment of society.

Some might argue that we should focus solely on solving problems on Earth, but the two efforts are not mutually exclusive. Technological advancements in space exploration will drive progress in all areas of society. It's a universal law of human history: progress in one field often leads to advancements in others.

The truth is that the future of human civilization relies on space colonization and addressing climate change with holistic data-driven solutions. The challenges of sustaining a growing global population can be mitigated by expanding beyond Earth and creating more sustainable methods of agriculture, energy production, and consumerism. While these tasks are immense, starting now is essential for ensuring the survival and prosperity of future generations. The decisions we make today will determine the world our descendants inherit. As we face the next great phase of technological expansion, it is clear that a science-driven government must be a central part of that effort, pushing humanity toward a brighter future.

Comments on All the Commas in Politics

A common rallying cry, especially from the progressive left, is the idea of overturning Citizens United, the landmark Supreme Court decision that equates money with speech. This ruling essentially permits private individuals to spend vast sums of money through political action committees (PACs) and super PACs on political campaigns, allowing millions—even billions of dollars to influence elections. While it is true that the Citizens United decision has been detrimental to the democratic process, reversing it is unlikely to achieve much. Even if a movement were to gather enough political power to overturn the decision, it would only create a shadow economy for political influence. The same wealthy individuals who fund PACs today would still find ways to wield their power behind the scenes, maintaining their anonymity but continuing to shape politics in vast ways.

Instead of attempting the impractical task of removing money from politics, we should focus on regulating it more effectively. The idea is not to eliminate political contributions but to shine a light on them. The current reporting systems are imperfect, but they offer a foundation that can be improved. The goal should be to create transparency around the influence of money—whether in the form of campaign contributions, lavish gifts, vacations, or other perks—towards elected and appointed officials across all levels and branches of government, from the executive branch to the judiciary.

Some critics argue that such laws would be burdensome, but the truth is that public officials should have no shame in reporting the gifts and contributions they receive, as long as those gifts are disclosed properly. And if an official just refuses the gifts and contributions then the effort becomes very easy. In truth, the transparency of these relationships is a benefit to democracy. If a politician receives significant campaign donations from the oil industry, they should openly acknowledge it and continue to support policies that align with those interests. This openness allows voters to make informed decisions about their representatives and whether their leader is supporting the right industries. One critical aside is that there should be no shame for elected officials that fully disclose their corruption because the people have a mechanism to correct that behavior if they so choose. However, for appointed officials like Secretaries or Supreme court justices, a different standard has to be applied, or the people need direct oversight of those individuals as well. At the very least, we should know what could be influencing our leaders.

Furthermore, closing the revolving door between public office and lobbying groups is crucial. The same way that non-compete agreements ensure the integrity of private companies, a "cool-off" period should exist for public officials who transition to lobbying roles. This cooling-off period is necessary for maintaining the integrity of our democratic system. When public officials leave office, they should no longer wield undue influence over policy decisions, another aspect of the immune system of our society which protects us against the undue influence of powerful, moneyed interests.

Ultimately, we need to focus on transparency and accountability, not on removing money from politics. The reality is that money has always influenced politics, from the days when industrialists like John D. Rockefeller and Joseph Kennedy used their wealth to gain power by installing their children in government, to the modern era when donations to PACs and think tanks achieve the same ends. Rather than trying to eliminate money from politics altogether, we should ensure that its influence is visible, transparent, and subject to public scrutiny. Voters deserve to know where the money is coming from and how it's being used to shape their democracy. Transparency and accountability are the best ways to safeguard the health and vitality of our nation.

MAGA: The Dystopia Within Our Grasp

This framework for a principled republic is a drive towards a more perfect union. But as with all movements of change, there is a dissenting voice. If you claim allegiance to the principles of liberty, equity, and morality, as I do, then you stand in opposition to the MAGA Oligarchy. This Oligarchy, formed by Donald Trump and his supporters—including figures like JD Vance, Stephen Miller, Elon Musk and the Project 2025 crew—represents an un-American force determined to undo the vision of equality that America's forefathers established. These individuals aim to transform America into a nation where White American chauvinism dictates behavior, rather than creating an equal society. They seek an oligarchy where wealth and power define the societal structure, and anyone who doesn't conform to their narrow definition of "good" is excommunicated, removed, or deported. These ideas are completely contrary to the American ideals of liberty and democracy.

The MAGA Oligarchy spreads its message through propaganda, manipulating the history of our nation—a history of mistakes, poor decisions, and bad ideas—to serve their goals. They claim a white Christian America that has declined into a stew of chaos and bloodshed by amorphous brown monsters and their enablers. But America's strength lies in its multiculturalism, in its diversity of perspectives, and in its commitment to the rule of law and the democratic process. The vision of democracy we champion is one where people, not just corporations or political elites, hold power—a democracy that values individual freedom, consumer rights, dignity, and respect.

In reality, the MAGA Oligarchy represents a dangerous shift toward authoritarianism. They use modern media, technology, and the grievances of the most disadvantaged in society to distort the truth and brainwash people into believing that their movement represents a step forward. It creates a society like those in Russia or parts of Africa, where democratic values are disregarded, and the power of the strongman dominates.

Americans care deeply about individualism and the right to have a say in their government. They value liberty, equity, and democracy, and they reject any attempt to disenfranchise them in favor of an elite class. Unfortunately, some have been misled into thinking that an authoritarian leader can solve all their problems. This is a false promise- a lie designed to strip Americans of their most valuable possession: their ability to make choices. The same lie has been used for centuries in nations around the globe, many of which are considered our traditional enemies to the nation.

The framework seeks to protect and nurture the American spirit, fostering a society where every individual is empowered to make decisions for themselves. The MAGA Oligarchy demands the surrender of that spirit, compelling people to give up their fundamental rights in exchange for the false security of authoritarian rule. If you are a patriotic American, you will stand opposed to the MAGA Oligarchy and everything it stands for.

Our Best Weapons: Compassion and Peace

There are few times in human history when true inflection points occur. There are moments when the right ingredients exist for absolute chaos, but also the ingredients for blissful ascent. I think we're living through one of those times today.

In writing the second edition of this book, we've experienced this period marked by the death of Charlie Kirk. When you look at the reality of political violence in America over the past couple of years, the pattern to me is very plain to see. If you go far enough to the right or far enough to the left, you end up in the same place.

The term "Nazi" is actually a shortening of two German words, which in English translate to "national socialism." Yet today, we call people on the right nazis, and we call people on the left socialists. If you go far enough on the left and listen to the Antifa movement, they are as militant as those who stormed the Capitol on January 6th, who were on the far right.

The death of Charlie Kirk illuminated the reality of our situation: we have principles, policies, and debates all exist within the crucible that is the American experiment. By way of free speech, by way of the freedoms that our Bill of Rights provides, and by way of our political system, we engage in those debates through our political culture in an effort to shape the society we want. We may disagree on what we want, but we find common elements.

But there is also hatred, dysfunction, and a sense of righteousness that takes hold when people go too far down that rabbit hole. The result is a desire for violence. The result is a nihilism that believes the only way out is death.

In The Art of War, Sun Tzu talks about many types of terrain—entangled terrain, critical terrain—which require different maneuvers in order to extricate yourself or overcome your enemy. Sometimes, overcoming your enemy means simply surviving. But there is another kind of terrain called "death terrain," where the only way out is through. You have to fight, and you are likely to die, but that is the only solution.

America is not there. Despite whatever hatred may come from individuals like Charlie Kirk, we have not reached that point. We have never been in death terrain—at least not for 150 years.

Our greatest weapon in this struggle is compassion—discussing ideals, debate and discourse, and trying to connect on a human level. We will disagree on policy, but the wild opportunity we have is to actually talk about those policies and ideals and what we care about.

There are many people who believe the world is unsalvageable, that the problems are too big, that the people in power are too powerful, and that there is nothing left to do. So the logic becomes: if you can't beat them, join them—or kill them.

To those people—if you are on the precipice of becoming one of them, or have already gone down that route—what I urge, what I pray for, is compassion. Radical compassion toward your enemy, toward those you disagree with, is the most powerful tool we have—the most powerful weapon against the dark future that could befall us.

We do not have to go down that nihilistic route. We can overcome the differences and divisions of our time. Hate is not the solution, neither is violence, nor is death. You do not have to abandon your values simply because you think no one can hear you.

For, when you express compassion toward others, when you express love and openness, it comes back to you. And that truth is a choice. When someone else is compassionate and open toward you, you must be compassionate and open toward them. When they ask, "What do you think? What does this make you feel?" you should ask the same in return.

I firmly believe most people believe in the same things. We just express them in different language, shaped by different experiences, interpretations of history, and educational backgrounds. We have different stories we like to tell, but they all have the same moral. We are all striving for the same future.

Only if we let each other speak—only if we give each other the space to explain ourselves—can we truly see that reality.

This is not a time we have experienced in generations. The particulars of this age will not fit perfectly with any historical echo—and that is also our advantage. Because no other time in human history has given us the power, we have to now write our own path. We can communicate, display, and distill information in ways our ancestors could only have imagined as the tools of gods.

Let us use those powers for the betterment of ourselves and each other. Let us find a pathway forward through this critical terrain before us. Let the hate die with the past.

Our Best Stratagem

One last item, as I write this in the late summer of 2025, it is becoming more and more apparent that the MAGA Oligarchy lead by Donald Trump wants civil war. They want political unrest. They want chaos. Those of us who wish to preserve America and all it stands for have one singular action to take: do nothing. We cannot protest or riot. We cannot be violent. We must express compassion, speak our minds and vote.

Peace is the weapon that will bring down this regime because violence is a ladder they will use to consolidate power. Our best strategy to win this civil war is not to fight the battles. This regime is like Ebola; it will create mass devastation, but it will burn itself out because of how much damage it does so quickly. There will be pain. Some people we know, and love will be hurt. Retribution will come later when we win. This will be the hardest task most of us ever do. But we must stay peaceful.

-PART TWO-

AN ACTION PLAN

High atop a hilltop clearing
A stalwart elm stands a-shining
Perched upon a branch arising
Alex Hummingbird sits surmising

Wondering wild through all he's seen
A falling elm and a rising king
He sits a-pondering what next he'll sing
What anthem could fix everything

What words with which to change the minds
Of every creature of elm-kind
Now how does he communicate
that in their hands is their fate?

Pathways to Progress

High ideals give comfort to the dreamers, but it is their translation into action that matters to voters.

What follows is a series of short discussions and policy suggestions designed to demonstrate the practical application of our new political framework. This framework is built on principles that seek to develop novel, holistic, and pragmatic solutions to the most pressing political challenges of our time—solutions that do not compromise equity, morality, or liberty.

That said, reality is complex. Part of my aim in presenting these discussions is to illustrate the nuanced context often missing from modern political discourse. This absence of nuance stifles progress. The framework I propose tackles complexity head-on, appropriately centering every issue around its impact on the individual, society, and the species as a whole—

through the lens of data and facts. Secular realities and verifiable truths serve as the basis for these solutions.

Some of my proposals may seem radical. Indeed, the most radical ideas are often addressing the hardest challenges in our current political climate. I do not pretend that change will come easily; on the contrary, the opposition to such ideas will be formidable. Yet I believe, with conviction, that this country possesses a unique immune system capable of overcoming entrenched corruption and dysfunction. If we persist, by fighting for what is just and right, then long-term success is not only possible, but inevitable.

These solutions, then, serve two purposes. First, they show that this framework can uncover policies worth pursuing and negotiating for because they could deliver enormous long-term value by advancing a principled, equitable, and moral republic. The second purpose is to inspire a new platform for reform in the United States. We do not have to cling to old dogmas. Despite what politicians and pundits may claim, fresh, innovative ideas exist.

The policies I present are not perfect, nor do I expect them all to become reality. But I want to get you thinking, talking, and imagining. In a democracy, every solution—no matter how radical or unconventional—should be put into consideration, debated, and refined by the crowd. That is how democracy works. That is how innovation works. That is how stagnation gives way to progress.

Of course, our nation is far too large for everyone to participate in a single discussion, and the challenges we face are too intricate to solve overnight. However, the goal here is to shift the national conversation toward a solution-based mindset. There is a way forward that transcends traditional liberal or conservative paradigms—a true third way rooted in equity, morality, and liberty in ways the current establishment cannot match. This framework provides a philosophical infrastructure to stand against mediocrity. It proves that solutions exist, can work, and are worth fighting for. And perhaps, through conversations like these, even better solutions no one has yet imagined will emerge.

The intention is simple: to get the conversation flowing toward a better path, whether it adopts this framework or another. The time for innovation is now.

The Prosperity Economy

For the past 80 years, the world has been misled by a dominant school of economics that fails to address economic reality while giving an excuse for economic extortion. The standard school of economics has failed to align with the true forces driving economic growth and stability. The framework redefines economic policy, fostering a system that genuinely supports prosperity and stability for all.

A foundational belief of the current economic paradigm, taught to students from a young age, is that the economy must cycle through booms and busts, with inherent winners and losers. This worldview accepts inequality as inevitable—some will always be at the top while others are relegated to the bottom. Communism, as conceptualized by Marx, challenged this notion, envisioning a system without stark divisions between an aristocratic elite and a laboring class. However, Marx's ideal has never been fully implemented. Historical attempts in countries like Russia and China have deviated significantly from his vision, largely because his model defies certain aspects of human nature, rendering it impractical.

Despite this, society can strive toward a more equitable framework akin to idealized socialism. Such a system could ensure that people's basic needs are met, allowing them to lead fulfilling lives. In this vision, middle-class life is marked by financial stability, access to essential resources, and the freedom to pursue personal and professional aspirations. Individuals would have opportunities to save, make meaningful purchases, and enjoy leisure without excessive work hours or constant financial stress. Children would grow up with access to education, healthcare, and mobility, ensuring they can build their own futures. In this society, being an artist wouldn't mean starving, and dedicating oneself to meaningful work wouldn't require endless toil.

This vision doesn't necessitate a revolutionary overhaul but rather a realignment of existing systems. Prosperity should be an intentional outcome of the economy, not a byproduct. Achieving this requires a shift in mindset among policymakers, economists, and corporate leaders. By adopting a framework centered on shared prosperity, society can build an economy designed to benefit everyone, not just those at the top.

At its core, the prosperity economy acknowledges three key agents: consumers, owners, and the government. Consumers include both working individuals, who earn a paycheck and use their income to meet personal needs, and consuming entities, which consume resources such as utilities, raw materials, equipment, and human expertise to produce goods and services. These could be small businesses, corporations, non-profits, NGOs, or government offices. Owners represent stakeholders who hold assets and manage resources within the economy. The government serves as the body responsible for establishing policies and systems that regulate and support economic activity, ensuring a balanced and thriving environment for all participants.

Consuming entities, in particular, rely on the time and intellect of working consumers to achieve their goals. This transactional relationship underscores the importance of fair compensation. If individuals dedicate their time to the needs of corporations or other entities, they should be rewarded in a way that allows them to thrive personally.

The second key agent in the economy is the owners who control the means of production. Owners include individuals or entities that possess corporations, debt, shares in companies, or other controlling interests. Often, executives should be considered owners, as they oversee and manage these assets. Owners occupy a unique role within the economy, distinct from that of consumers. While owners may consume as individuals, their primary responsibility in their role as owners is ensuring the longevity and success of their assets. This includes adhering to regulations and fulfilling their responsibilities within the broader social contract of corporate citizenship.

Owners have a duty to align their actions with the requirements and principles set by the government and society. This concept, known as corporate citizenship, underscores the interconnectedness between ownership and societal obligations. Corporate entities must contribute positively to the economic system, adhering to rules that ensure fairness, stability, and sustainability. When corporations shun duties as citizens, they harm individuals and society. For too long, government and consumers have allowed abuses by corporations on the grounds that their products are useful, and the organizations drive economic growth. The truth is that market economics ensures no product or service from one company cannot be replaced by another. When we start holding corporations to a moral standard through our employment, investment, and purchasing choices, we will begin to reshape the fabric of our civilization for the better.

Traditionally, governments have been seen as stimulators of economic growth, often by prioritizing corporate support. This approach, rooted in conservative economic ideology, emphasizes boosting corporations to fuel the economy. However, a truly prosperous economy emerges when consumers—both individuals and entities—have sufficient cash flow to meet their needs and engage in discretionary spending. The hard fact is that economic growth is driven by consumer activity: when people spend, demand rises, leading to increased production, job creation, and overall economic expansion. The more cash consumers have, the more they can participate in the economy, sustaining the cycle of growth and maturity.

To that end, the government's primary role in the prosperity economy is to prevent the exploitation of consumers, ensuring that the marketplace remains fair and trustworthy. This responsibility includes maintaining fair pricing so that goods and services reflect their true value, upholding quality assurance to ensure that products and services meet promised standards and deliver genuine benefits while safeguarding against deceptive practices. For instance, if a consumer spends $1,000 on a medication that proves to be a cheap placebo, they have been exploited, and it is the government's duty to prevent such occurrences. In truth if a consumer is forced to pay $1,000 for a monopolized medication, the consumer is still being exploited. Additionally, the government must protect environmental and institutional systems, which are essential to the well-being and sustainability of society. Corporations and other entities will always push the boundaries of what society will allow in order to meet their needs. In the name of universal morality, governments must put hard guardrails against environmental and social exploitation otherwise current and future generations will find their world inhospitable.

With this context, it is important that we understand that the government is a unique economic agent, distinct from corporations, owners, and consumers. Its role is twofold: to protect against exploitation and ensure equitable economic participation while maintaining its obligations through responsible fiscal management. By balancing these responsibilities, the government ensures a stable and fair economy that benefits all participants.

By protecting consumers and ensuring fair economic practices, the government creates an environment where both consumers and owners can thrive, fostering a stable and prosperous economy. After all, consumers have the freedom to spend their money as they wish, but the government must ensure that a consumer's choices do not lead to danger or harm. A good example of this principle in action is gun regulation. In the United States, consumers have the right to purchase firearms. However, this freedom must be balanced with safeguards to prevent exploitation that could harm society, such as mass shootings. The government's role is not to demonize guns but to address the misuse of such items when they are exploited for destructive purposes. For example, restricting access to military-grade weapons like M16s and AR-15s is a way to prevent their use in mass violence. Without such restrictions, law enforcement faces an uphill battle, needing to contend with increasingly powerful weapons, which endanger not just the public but also officers themselves. In this sense, regulation protects the broader institutions like law enforcement and public safety that would otherwise be undermined by unchecked exploitation of dangerous goods.

Importantly, governments impose rules on corporations and their owners to ensure product quality and safety. For instance, pharmaceutical companies must ensure their medications are effective and safe, preventing harm or fraud. While companies have the freedom to sell their products, they must adhere to standards that protect the public from harm. The same principle applies to economic equity. Exploitation can also occur when wages are too low, denying workers fair compensation. Through mechanisms like OSHA regulations or union protections, governments can level the playing field and uphold fairness in the economy.

One of the critical concepts to grasp when discussing economic structures and policies is the importance of enabling consumers—both individuals and entities—to have greater access to free cash. The foundation of this approach is the understanding that when working individuals and businesses have more disposable income, the economy as a whole becomes stronger.

What does this look like in practice? For consumers,

it might mean higher wages or lower interest rates to access capital more easily. For corporations, it could involve policies that provide more affordable borrowing options. Other measures might include universal basic income (UBI) or government-supported stipends to ensure that everyone has a financial safety net.

Critics often label such policies as "socialist," but this is a misrepresentation rooted in capitalist propaganda. The notion that UBI or government-mandated minimum wages equate to socialism is a deliberate distortion designed to preserve the status quo. Why? Because if everyday people have more disposable income, they gain autonomy, and that challenges the entrenched power structures. In contrast, when people are poor, they are more pliable, angrier, and less likely to resist the narratives fed to them. This dynamic feeds into the political paradigm, allowing those in power to exploit societal instability to maintain control.

True socialism, by definition, involves government ownership of the means of production—factories, resources, and industries. In a socialist economy, the government dictates what gets produced, at what cost, and whether those goods are sold or distributed freely. Countries like China illustrate genuine socialist principles, where the government owns a stake in most major companies, particularly those providing essential goods or services. These companies are required to meet production quotas to fulfill public needs, often at cost. Any surplus production can then be sold for profit. This approach ensures basic needs are met while allowing for private enterprise—a blend of socialism and capitalism that has fueled China's economic growthxviii. In contrast, policies like UBI or higher minimum wages are about ensuring equitable access to financial resources fostering economic mobility and opportunity. UBI and related ideas aim to empower individuals by providing them with a financial foundation, not by taking ownership of production. These measures address systemic issues such as homelessness, student debt, and healthcare or childcare inequities, which are symptoms of a society that fails to provide its citizens with the tools they need to prosper.

Opponents argue that programs like UBI encourage irresponsibility, but evidence suggests otherwise. "[A] study in Stockton, California, found that full-time employment increased because UBI gave people time to apply for better jobs, rather than having to work multiple part-time jobs. And a study in Hudson, New York, found that all employment increased from 29 to 63 percent, which contradicts opponents of UBI that claim it would "destroy" any incentive to work."xix In my experience, most people, given the opportunity, want to lead productive lives. They want stable jobs, education, healthcare, and the means to build a future. The problem lies in systemic barriers that make these aspirations unattainable for many. By creating policies that alleviate these barriers—such as affordable healthcare, accessible education, and fair wages—we can unlock the potential of individuals and, by extension, the broader economy.

The current welfare system in the United States often fails its beneficiaries, offering limited assistance while imposing stringent, sometimes demeaning, requirements. This perpetuates cycles of poverty rather than breaking them. A reimagined system should prioritize dignity, accessibility, and opportunity. For instance, offering universal healthcare and basic income could ensure that no one has to choose between rent and medical bills or between education and survival. Providing these opportunities is not about forcing choices or dictating lifestyles. It is about ensuring that every individual has the foundation to make their own decisions. People who feel supported and secure are more likely to contribute positively to society, whether through work, innovation, or community engagement. Even those who initially misuse their financial support, for example by spending it on harmful habits, deserve the chance to access resources that could help them turn their lives around. Investing in people isn't just morally right, it's economically sound. Ensuring that basic needs like housing, food, and healthcare are met leads to a healthier, more educated, and more productive populace. The historical evidence suggests that with healthy and productive consumer class, crime rates decrease, GDP rises, and societal happiness improves. With access to opportunities, individuals are more likely to seek fulfillment through work and creativity, driving economic growth and innovation.

We need leaders who understand that government is not about controlling the people but empowering them. By providing the tools for people to live stable, productive lives, we can create a society where everyone has the chance to thrive. This isn't socialism, nor is it pure capitalism—it's populism. It's a prosperity economy that values people as its greatest resource, ensuring that no one is left behind. By centering economic policies on equity and opportunity, we can build a healthier, more resilient society for generations to come.

Media and Social Media

The United States has a well-documented media problem. For the better part of a decade, the right wing has attacked the media, branding it as "fake news." While I don't believe the mainstream media is fabricating stories, Fox News being a notable exception, the real issue lies elsewhere. The problem isn't outright fabrication; it's the "entertainment-ization" of the news. News media has become unserious, overly biased, and dysfunctional, failing to fulfill its critical role in a democracy.

To address this issue, we first need to define what role the media should play. Many people question whether we even need traditional media in the age of the internet, where access to primary sources is often just a click away. Personally, I prefer reading direct press releases or watching press conferences over relying on a journalist's summary. The modern internet ecosystem makes primary sources more accessible, but it also amplifies opinions and misinformation. Social media, by design, is an inappropriate platform for consuming news. The platforms purposely create an echo chamber where people only see what aligns with their beliefs. The algorithms prioritize sensationalism, often at the expense of accuracy. Citizens must recognize this and treat social media like a Netflix series or an art gallery—entertaining but not necessarily real. In truth, this issue with social media is not limited to professional news content. Even personal posts are curated to show the best version of reality, and we must remind ourselves (and our children) that what we see online is often a blend of fact and fiction. When it comes to news or informational posts, we have no reliable way to verify their accuracy, and the rise of AI has made policing misinformation effectively impossible.

The solution begins with personal responsibility: treating social media as a source of entertainment rather than information. Governments and political leaders should also step up by releasing press statements through official websites and legitimate media outlets rather than social platforms. However, this brings us to the larger issue: the broken state of traditional media. Major broadcasters and newspapers face economic challenges, largely due to the internet and the decline of print media. Ad revenue, once their lifeblood, is increasingly unreliable and often compromises journalistic integrity when corporate interests are involved.

The central question is how to ensure a free, independent media that isn't beholden to corporate or political power. One potential solution, ironically, is a government-run news outlet. While state media raises concerns—particularly when we look at authoritarian regimes—an American version could be structured differently. Such an outlet would focus exclusively on reporting verified events, steering clear of personalities and opinions. It would operate under strict bipartisan oversight, with commissioners appointed from all branches of government to prevent political bias. Its stories would be fully transparent, subject to Freedom of Information requests to ensure accountability within certain limits to protect the confidentiality of sources – a paradigm borrowed from the Department of Defense. This state media would be one entity within the larger media landscape that would provide verifiably factual information with a controlled level of bias.

Another approach could involve creating a tax structure for news organizations. Outlets that register as official news organizations could receive tax benefits similar to nonprofits. This financial support could reduce their reliance on corporate funding, fostering marginally greater independence. In exchange, these organizations would be held to strict standards of factual reporting. They would need to back up their stories with verifiable sources, and failure to do so would result in severe penalties, including potential loss of their registered status.

These measures could help rebuild trust in the media by ensuring that factual reporting is prioritized. Citizens who prefer primary sources could rely on a government-run site for raw information, while other outlets could build on this foundation. Ultimately, fixing the media landscape requires both systemic reforms and a cultural shift. People must approach all media, whether traditional or social, with critical thinking and an acknowledgement of some bias. By fostering a system that rewards accuracy and punishes misinformation, we can take a meaningful step toward addressing the severe problems in today's media environment. All that being said, the troubles with the media in the United States is a complex and nuanced issue that even these framework solutions imperfectly address. The best solution comes down to personal choices about platforms and sources, astuteness to the biases that exist, and a practice of critical thought, data driven research, and a trust but verify mentality.

Foreign Policy

When you think about your life and your everyday existence you don't necessarily think about how the United States operates on the world stage. Yet, at the same time, the most frightening scenarios of our time are almost entirely born from other countries.

On a daily basis, threats come to us from the news media and from politicians. These threats exist in various forms but often take the shape of some country trying to undermine us, harm us, or destabilize other parts of the world. As of this writing, we see the Russia-Ukraine war, ongoing conflict in the Middle East, and numerous other areas of instability that pose potential threats to the U.S. We're also witnessing a border crisis, with millions of people entering the country. There is a non-zero chance that some of these individuals have malicious intentions, whether as operatives or terrorists with an agenda to harm civilians. This reality makes discussions about immigration, democracy, governance, and economics inseparable from the critical aspects of foreign policy.

At the same time, we must reckon with the truth about America's role in the world. For roughly the past century, the United States has acted as both a force for good and, undeniably, a bully. We gained immense international power in the 20th century, using it to subject other populations to fear and death under the guise of defeating nebulous enemies like communism and terrorism. While these threats were real, their scale and nature did not always warrant the overwhelming responses the U.S. delivered[ii].

A new paradigm for America must begin with a foreign policy that acknowledges the horrors we have inflicted globally, much like those of past empires, such as the British or other European powers. While we are not alone in being a force of negative impact, we are the most recent and often the most egregious abuser in certain parts of the world, particularly the Middle East and Southeast Asia.

Any principled foreign policy framework must start with two core truths. First, every nation has the undeniable right to its own sovereignty—the freedom to govern itself, make its own choices, and carve out its path without outside interference. Second, no country has the right to infringe on the sovereignty of another. These principles are simple but powerful, and they lay the foundation for a world where respect and equity guide the relationships between nations.

To illustrate the principle of sovereignty, imagine living next to a neighbor with different values and practices. Perhaps they are devoutly religious while you're secular, perhaps they raise their children differently, or treat their pets in ways you don't agree with. So long as these practices are not abusive or illegal, it isn't your place to impose your values on them. Similarly, if they try to impose their beliefs on you, it will justifiably lead to conflict. This metaphor extends to the global stage: nations have the right to self-determination and violating that right creates unnecessary and often destructive conflict.

However, this respect for sovereignty doesn't mean nations can't share opinions or encourage better practices. Just as neighbors might advise each other in good faith, countries can suggest improvements or offer assistance. But forcing change—through invasion or coercion—crosses a line that no nation has the right to cross.

Immigration adds another layer to this conversation. Nations must allow people dissatisfied with their government's policies to leave and seek better opportunities elsewhere. For the U.S., as a pluralistic society with a secular government and multicultural heritage, it is our duty to provide a haven for those who align with our values within the logistical boundaries of our nation. Conversely, we must respect those who prefer to remain in their home country and those who emigrate to nations with different values than ourselves.

This exchange of people and ideas is vital to respecting sovereignty on a human level. Some will choose to leave societies they find oppressive, just as others may gravitate toward stricter or more homogeneous societies. Both choices are valid and must be respected.

Finally, the U.S. must accept that its values do not universally apply. Other parts of the world, Middle east being the best example, operate within a different latticework of cultural and historical contexts that our Western perspective cannot unravel. Conflicts in these regions often stem from deep-seated issues that do not align with the American or European understanding of nationhood, governance, and society[vi].

While individuals may hold strong personal opinions shaped by their cultural or religious heritage, the U.S. government should take on a more universalist approach that emphasizes global security, regional sovereignty, and humanitarian values. An honest review of history and current events makes clear that conflicts in the Middle East are primarily shaped by two forces: ancient cultural divisions and external interference. For centuries, rivalries such as those between Jews and Arabs, Sunnis and Shiites, as well as tribal disputes, have shaped the landscape of the region. These conflicts are deeply ingrained and not easily resolved, often fueled by generational grievances and cultural identities that are difficult for outsiders to fully understand. In addition, Western powers, particularly throughout the 20th and 21st centuries, have played a role in exacerbating these tensions through interventions, colonialism, and strategic alliances that have caused resentment among local populations. This history of meddling has contributed to the persistent instability and division in the region, making it clear that foreign powers cannot solve the problems of the Middle East[vi].

The powerful nations of the world, including the United States, must adopt a policy best described as Middle East Determinism. This approach is not about abandoning responsibility but about recognizing the limits of foreign involvement. This means that while these powers can maintain trade agreements and provide humanitarian assistance, they should refrain from intervening in the region's political or military affairs. The countries of the Middle East have the resources, knowledge, and capacity to work through their conflicts. However, they need the space to do so without the distractions of foreign intervention or the imposition of external agendas.

A key component of this policy is providing humanitarian aid in a fair and equitable manner. Given the inevitable civilian casualties and displacement caused by conflicts, the international community must ensure that aid reaches all affected areas without taking sides. Humanitarian assistance should be coordinated globally with contributions from all major powers. This collective approach ensures that aid is provided where it is most needed without political bias or the reinforcement of existing power structures.

While non-interference is the cornerstone of this policy, there are areas where international cooperation remains essential, particularly regarding nuclear proliferation. While the Middle Eastern nations, as with any conflict region such as South Asia, Africa, or central America, should be allowed to determine their political futures, the global community must intervene to prevent the escalation of Weapons of Mass Destruction, genocides and other crimes against humanity. This is an area where collective action can help maintain stability and security in the region without infringing on the sovereignty of nations.

As an aside, the use and threat of nuclear force, systematic genocide, holocaust, and the use of biological weapons are mistakes and scars that the people of the most powerful nations of the world must bear—proliferation against these things for all other nations is about saving humanity from repeating these mistakes. There is no need for history to continue to be scarred in these ways.

Ultimately, humanity shares common desires: safety, opportunity, and the freedom to live fulfilling lives.

Different nations and cultures may pursue these goals in different ways, and that's okay. We must recognize that our model of governance is not universally applicable, as is no one else's. By respecting the sovereignty of others and refraining from imposing our respective values, humanity can foster a world where mutual understanding and cooperation thrive. This is the path to a more peaceful and equitable global future.

Healthcare

Immigration remains one of the most hotly debated issues in the United States, and it has raised significant concerns about national sovereignty, security, and the country's future. The framework for addressing immigration in the U.S. holds several truths to be self-evident. First, securing the nation's borders is vital. A country must have a controlled, legal immigration process to protect its sovereignty and national security. Without this, the very foundations of the nation are compromised, and that is unacceptable.

However, another key truth about immigration into this country is that it is no accident that our country is the ideal destination. It is not merely about changing demographics, although that is a factor. The United States has always been a land of possibility—a beacon of hope for people from all over the world. Immigrants come here for the same reasons the English Puritans did centuries ago. They are drawn by the promise of a better life, free from political persecution, economic hardship, or social constraints that exist in their home countries.

The U.S. has always attracted people seeking a better life because of its reputation for social mobility, democracy, and a thriving economy where hard work and skills lead to success. While other places in the world may offer freedom and opportunity, few have the resources, space, and land that America does. Furthermore, the United States has a long history of multiculturalism. Unlike other nations built on a single culture or religion, America's strength lies in its diversity—a melting pot that brings together people from different backgrounds to create a rich, vibrant society in which anyone from anywhere can find their community. This is a strength that must not be compromised.

Yet, while the United States is a land of opportunity, we must also protect our sovereignty and security. There are risks involved, particularly from those who may wish to do us harm or undermine the nation. Some may be motivated by political ideologies or by resentment over U.S. foreign policies. This reality cannot be ignored. Therefore, the solution must be twofold: on one hand, the U.S. must maintain a secure and controlled immigration system; on the other, it must continue to be a place that welcomes those who seek a better life.

The first step is to modernize the immigration system, bringing it into the 21st century. The U.S. must become the easiest country on the planet to immigrate to legally and digitally. This means investing in border patrol and law enforcement at both the borders and ports of entry. The U.S. must enhance the capabilities of Customs and Border Protection, providing them with the technology, drones, and personnel needed to ensure constant surveillance of the borders and detect illegal activity. At the same time, there must be a digital, streamlined visa application system that makes it easy for individuals to apply and track their progress.

To make the process of immigrating to the U.S. more efficient, the system would involve gathering essential information from applicants, including an in-country address, and providing documentation to verify their identity and status including a recent photo taken from the application (so they cannot upload an altered picture). Once an application is submitted, it would automatically verify through various law enforcement databases to ensure the person has no criminal or terrorist connections. If the individual is flagged from the automatic system, they are barred from entry until an official can review on appeal. Individuals who are approved would have their information checked upon arrival at the border including an onsite facial scan that matches against the picture using AI technology. Nothing about this approach is technologically impractical and the entire system can be secured and integrated with Customs and Border Patrol at every border station, port and airport. Moreover, mobile access could be created for officers on patrol that catch illegal crossers.

Upon crossing the border and passing verification, individuals would have 90 days to prove they have a job, a school to attend, or have a visa or green card. If they, or their children, fail to meet these requirements, they could be deported, with possible exceptions for certain circumstances, such as political asylum or in progress visa applications. They would need to pay taxes and re-register on an annual basis to maintain their status, but they would be required to apply for permanent residence after a certain amount of time. Those who violate the rules or commit crimes would face immediate deportation. If someone repeatedly tries to enter the country after being deported or is involved in criminal activities, they could be charged as an illegal infiltrator and face prison time before deportation as well as being banned from the country. All of this would be enforced through coordination with local and federal law enforcement and utilization of modern facial recognition technologies.

In addition, the U.S. must address the large number of undocumented individuals already in the country. A grace period would be provided for all immigrants, documented and undocumented, to enter their information into the new system, after which they would be subject to deportation if they fail to comply. Employers who knowingly hire undocumented workers, and do not help them to apply for this program, would be held accountable for unpaid taxes, and their workers would be deported and banned.

This system aims to strike a balance: maintaining the integrity and security of the nation while also allowing individuals who seek a better life to come to the U.S. legally and contribute to its society. By modernizing immigration, enhancing enforcement, and introducing consequences for violations, the U.S. can continue to be a land of opportunity while safeguarding its future.

Immigration

Immigration remains one of the most hotly debated issues in the United States, and it has raised significant concerns about national sovereignty, security, and the country's future. The framework for addressing immigration in the U.S. holds several truths to be self-evident. First, securing the nation's borders is vital. A country must have a controlled, legal immigration process to protect its sovereignty and national security. Without this, the very foundations of the nation are compromised, and that is unacceptable.

However, another key truth about immigration into this country is that it is no accident that our country is the ideal destination. It is not merely about changing demographics, although that is a factor. The United States has always been a land of possibility—a beacon of hope for people from all over the world. Immigrants come here for the same reasons the English Puritans did centuries ago. They are drawn by the promise of a better life, free from political persecution, economic hardship, or social constraints that exist in their home countries.

The U.S. has always attracted people seeking a better life because of its reputation for social mobility, democracy, and a thriving economy where hard work and skills lead to success. While other places in the world may offer freedom and opportunity, few have the resources, space, and land that America does. Furthermore, the United States has a long history of multiculturalism. Unlike other nations built on a single culture or religion, America's strength lies in its diversity—a melting pot that brings together people from different backgrounds to create a rich, vibrant society in which anyone from anywhere can find their community. This is a strength that must not be compromised.

Yet, while the United States is a land of opportunity, we must also protect our sovereignty and security. There are risks involved, particularly from those who may wish to do us harm or undermine the nation. Some may be motivated by political ideologies or by resentment over U.S. foreign policies. This reality cannot be ignored. Therefore, the solution must be twofold: on one hand, the U.S. must maintain a secure and controlled immigration system; on the other, it must continue to be a place that welcomes those who seek a better life.

The first step is to modernize the immigration system, bringing it into the 21st century. The U.S. must become the easiest country on the planet to immigrate to legally and digitally. This means investing in border patrol and law enforcement at both the borders and ports of entry. The U.S. must enhance the capabilities of Customs and Border Protection, providing them with the technology, drones, and personnel needed to ensure constant surveillance of the borders and detect illegal activity. At the same time, there must be a digital, streamlined visa application system that makes it easy for individuals to apply and track their progress.

To make the process of immigrating to the U.S. more efficient, the system would involve gathering essential information from applicants, including an in-country address, and providing documentation to verify their identity and status including a recent photo taken from the application (so they cannot upload an altered picture). Once an application is submitted, it would automatically verify through various law enforcement databases to ensure the person has no criminal or terrorist connections. If the individual is flagged from the automatic system, they are barred from entry until an official can review on appeal. Individuals who are approved would have their information checked upon arrival at the border including an onsite facial scan that matches against the picture using AI technology. Nothing about this approach is technologically impractical and the entire system can be secured and integrated with Customs and Border Patrol at every border station, port and airport. Moreover, mobile access could be created for officers on patrol that catch illegal crossers.

Upon crossing the border and passing verification, individuals would have 90 days to prove they have a job, a school to attend, or have a visa or green card. If they, or their children, fail to meet these requirements, they could be deported, with possible exceptions for certain circumstances, such as political asylum or in progress visa applications. They would need to pay taxes and re-register on an annual basis to maintain their status, but they would be required to apply for permanent residence after a certain amount of time. Those who violate the rules or commit crimes would face immediate deportation. If someone repeatedly tries to enter the country after being deported or is involved in criminal activities, they could be charged as an illegal infiltrator and face prison time before deportation as well as being banned from the country. All of this would be enforced through coordination with local and federal law enforcement and utilization of modern facial recognition technologies.

In addition, the U.S. must address the large number of undocumented individuals already in the country. A grace period would be provided for all immigrants, documented and undocumented, to enter their information into the new system, after which they would be subject to deportation if they fail to comply. Employers who knowingly hire undocumented workers, and do not help them to apply for this program, would be held accountable for unpaid taxes, and their workers would be deported and banned.

This system aims to strike a balance: maintaining the integrity and security of the nation while also allowing individuals who seek a better life to come to the U.S. legally and contribute to its society. By modernizing immigration, enhancing enforcement, and introducing consequences for violations, the U.S. can continue to be a land of opportunity while safeguarding its future.

Education

Education policy in the United States requires substantial reform. While the U.S. has historically been a leader in education, there are two glaring issues that demand immediate attention: primary school education and the way education is financed. Since the COVID-19 pandemic, there has been a well-documented decline in math and reading scores, which highlights broader systemic problems within public school systems.

Much of this comes down to funding. Public education in the U.S. has largely been treated as a state and local issue because federalizing such a massive system is incredibly challenging. While federal grant funds do filter down to schools, a universal federal solution for financing primary and high school education across the board isn't practical. That said, there are specific areas where the federal government can—and must—step in to help.

One critical area is early childhood education. It stands to reason that a child's early years lay the foundation for their entire educational journey. The most impactful education a child can receive often comes from their parents—through being read to, having meaningful conversations, and engaging with language in a full and authentic way. Children are biologically wired to process complex language, and the brain at that age acts as a sponge. When parents speak to their children as intelligent individuals, expose them to an expansive vocabulary, and nurture a love of reading and learning, those children develop cognitive and emotional tools that serve them for life.

As a society, we must understand that early childhood education is not just an academic phase—it's the bedrock of a child's future. If children grow up with a love of learning, they are more likely to engage in school, stay in school, and value education throughout their lives. This sets them up to contribute meaningfully to society and succeed as adults.

Beyond early education, we must ensure that the pipeline to adulthood prepares students to be productive members of society. A critical gap exists in areas such as personal finance education and sexual education, particularly at the high school level.

Personal finance classes, for example, are essential for

teaching teenagers how to budget, manage debt, and navigate adulthood. Similarly, comprehensive and secular sexual education—starting in middle school—must provide students with honest, factual information about biology, reproductive health, contraceptive methods, and consent. These courses cannot be watered down. Parents can and should instill their own values, but schools must ensure students have the knowledge they need to make informed decisions. Too often, a lack of proper education leaves young people unprepared and vulnerable. Knowledge is power, and providing this education empowers students to take control of their lives.

Additionally, we cannot neglect the role of arts, athletics, and social clubs in childhood development. Debate teams, theater clubs, and team sports teach essential life skills like collaboration, critical thinking, and discipline. Every child should experience these activities because they foster well-rounded individuals who are equipped to thrive in diverse environments.

Another major cultural shift we must address is the perception of success in education. Our society often treats the path from elementary school to college as the only legitimate route to adulthood. As a result, people who pursue vocational training or end up with a GED are unfairly stigmatized. This mindset is outdated and harmful. Education—whether academic or vocational—should prepare students to be productive adults in whatever form that takes.

To that end, there must be federal funding for vocational education programs. Employers must also eliminate unnecessary requirements for four-year degrees in entry-level jobs. A high school diploma should have real value in the marketplace, and students who choose to pursue trades must be supported.

At the same time, we must overhaul the student finance system to address the skyrocketing costs of higher education. Over the past few decades, tuition has risen to unsustainable levels, saddling graduates with crippling debt and limiting their social mobility. Many private universities operate as nonprofits yet maintain massive endowments while continuously raising tuition. Federal policy must ensure that universities utilize their endowments to support operational costs and prevent unjustifiable tuition hikes.

Furthermore, we need stronger loan forgiveness programs. A robust federal system—similar to the Public Service Loan Forgiveness program—should allow working graduates to have their loans forgiven over time. This would alleviate financial burdens and ensure education remains a tool for social and economic advancement, not a lifelong handicap. Obviously, paying the loan over its term would accomplish the same end result as the forgiveness. However, I have to push back on that as a functional solution for the simple reason that the rate at which a person can accrue student debt significantly outpaces the rate at which a person can accrue additional income. Most student debt loans are 10–20-year loans if not longer. The terms are akin to a mortgage loan. The difference is that mortgage debt creates a platform for wealth creation because equity accrues as the loan is paid off. However, student debt has no equity function as it is paid off despite having a similarly aggressive impact on monthly expenses. This asymmetry between income and wealth creation and the debt is why specialized, government programs need to provide additional relief for student borrowers. Furthermore, for the many people who have been able to pay off their loans the hard way, some kind of temporary tax credit program should be set up to ensure an equitable impact on these reforms.

At its core, education policy must focus on creating equitable access to learning opportunities, eliminating economic barriers, and supporting students from childhood to adulthood. Whether through better early childhood programs, personal finance classes, vocational pathways, or opportunities like improved teacher pay and benefits, free public university options, etc. the goal is the same: to ensure every child has the opportunity to succeed.

Our leaders must prioritize education as the foundation for a healthy, functional society. The dividends of investing in education are generational. It begins with how we talk to our children, how we engage them in learning, and how we structure our policies to value education as a mechanism for social mobility. If we build an education system that equips children with knowledge, skills, and confidence, we will create a stronger, more prosperous future for all.

Gun Rights

The United States has a gun problem. At the core of this issue lies the Second Amendment, which states that citizens have "the right to bear arms" and "form regulated militias."[xi] However, this amendment has been conflated and warped into an excuse for individual citizens to wage war against each other and increasingly threaten law enforcement. The Second Amendment guarantees a fundamental liberty: the right to own a gun. However, it does not provide for unlimited ownership of firearms, nor does it preclude government regulation.

The amendment was drafted by individuals living under occupation, facing a hostile force. They believed it was critical that the government could not completely disarm the citizenry. Additionally, they saw the necessity of self-defense during periods of lawlessness and conflict, such as the Indian Wars.

One oft neglected nuance is that the amendment explicitly references "regulated militias," which today are embodied in the National Guard and law enforcement from the FBI to local Sheriffs—not groups like the Proud Boys. The intent was to ensure that, if necessary, states could use organized forces to defend their citizens against tyranny. This does not mean individuals have unalienable rights to stockpile military-grade weapons and take up arms against law enforcement or the government. That interpretation is fundamentally flawed and undermines a functional society.

Some argue that government regulation infringes upon the Second Amendment, claiming there should be no restrictions on gun ownership. This is simply untrue. The Second Amendment does not grant unrestricted access to any kind of firearm. Its purpose is to prevent an asymmetry of power between the citizenry and the federal government by allowing for weapons at all levels of society. Furthermore, it provides for the general welfare of the population by allowing them to defend themselves whether from animals or bad actors in the context of their own property.

It is clear that the Founding Fathers recognized the need for checks against tyranny, but they also structured the Constitution to safeguard democracy. There is no constitutional pathway to dictatorship in the United States unlike in other democracies around the world. An overthrow of our constitutional government is easier if the federal military is the only entity with weapons. But the second amendment addresses this risk by ensuring that other regulated militias under the control of the people also have weapons. But this is secondary safeguard on purpose.

The first line of defense against tyranny is not the Second Amendment but the First Amendment. Free speech, the right to protest, a free press, and freedom of religion—these are the foundations that protect us from oppressive government. The Second Amendment, by contrast, is about entrusting the collective defense against tyranny to regulated militias like the National Guard and law enforcement. Critically, since the constitution did not design these agencies, the founders created a structure where individuals have right to arms and then must create their regulations accordingly. Remember, the founding father's core belief is that people can govern themselves and there is no language in the second amendment against regulating individual gun ownership.

Unfortunately, there are powerful forces who push for expansive gun rights, not out of concern for self-defense but to foster fear and profit. Why would anyone want armed citizen militias capable of confronting police or federal agents? The answer is intimidation. When fear is pervasive, people become more easily controlled.

More fear leads to more people needing self-defense, which lines the pockets of gun manufacturers and others in the industry—it's all a business model meant to keep the rich rich and the powerful in power.

Gun regulations in this country must be straightforward. The government has the right to regulate weapons—nowhere does the Second Amendment state otherwise. Weapons designed for self-defense should remain accessible to those people who are deemed qualified, but military-grade firearms like AR-15s do not meet that criteria. There is no scenario where such weapons are necessary for self-defense. While one might argue that superior firepower is needed to protect against an intruder, we, as a society, have already run that experiment. The result has not been self-defense; instead, military-grade firearms have been used to murder children and commit mass killings.

The consequences of this are clear. As a society, we must decide: is the mass murder of children acceptable? The answer must be no. Allowing unfettered access to weapons of war fundamentally restricts the liberty of victims, tilting power in favor of those who wield such weapons. There is no liberty in killing. We do not, as a free society, grant the right to murder. If we allow the continued proliferation of military-grade firearms, we must also accept a reality in which mass killings are normalized and unpunishable. But that is not the society we claim to want. That is not freedom, nor is it moral. If we value an equitable, just, and free society, we must make a collective decision to remove these weapons from our streets. We have already seen the horrendous consequences of failing to do so.

Criminal Justice

The United States has a complex and troubled history regarding criminal justice, marked by systemic challenges and long-standing issues. At the core of these challenges lies systemic racism, an undeniable and deeply ingrained element of American culture since the nation's founding. Addressing this foundational issue is essential for meaningful reform.

Another critical concern is the country's exceptionally high incarceration rate, much of which stems from outdated policies, such as those born out of the "war on drugs." These efforts have largely failed to curb drug use or rehabilitate offenders, instead perpetuating cycles of punishment without addressing root causes or fostering criminal reform.

To understand the broader issues, it's vital to reflect

on the purpose of criminal justice itself. Historically, the concept of imprisonment was rooted in reform and redemption. Institutions like Philadelphia's Eastern State Penitentiary in the 19th century aimed to rehabilitate individuals who posed problems to society, guiding them toward becoming moral and productive citizens. Over time, this original intent has eroded[xvi]. Today, the justice system often focuses on isolating individuals deemed harmful to society, with little regard for their potential for reform.

The reality of most criminal behavior underscores the flaws in this approach. A significant proportion of offenders are poor, driven to crime by desperation and systemic inequities. For many, their circumstances—lack of education, unstable family structures, and limited economic opportunities—leave them without viable paths to meet basic needs. Others suffer from mental health challenges that inhibit their ability to integrate into society or make rational decisions. These factors often push individuals into cycles of crime, further exacerbating their marginalization.

Beyond these social drivers, punitive measures like the death penalty highlight the inefficiencies and moral ambiguities of the current system. Despite its use for centuries, the death penalty has not proven to deter crime effectively. Moreover, the potential for miscarriages of justice—wrongful convictions due to flawed evidence, human error, or systemic biases—raises significant ethical concerns. The financial burden on taxpayers is another drawback, as inmates often spend decades on death row, accruing substantial costs for their incarceration and execution.

Alternatives, such as life imprisonment without parole, offer similar deterrence without the moral and practical complications of state-sponsored executions. Yet even these measures warrant scrutiny, as they reflect a broader societal decision to abandon the possibility of redemption for certain individuals.

Addressing the root causes of crime and recidivism requires systemic change. Most incarcerated individuals are not hardened criminals but people who have committed non-violent offenses or struggled with mental health issues. Their time in prison often compounds their disadvantages, leaving them ill-equipped to reenter society. Employers are hesitant to hire individuals with criminal records, further entrenching their economic struggles and increasing the likelihood of reoffending.

Reform must focus on two key areas. First, prisons should mandate education or vocational training for inmates serving sentences longer than one or two years. By obtaining degrees or certifications, individuals would have a greater chance of reintegrating into society upon release. Incentives such as reduced sentences or expunged records could encourage participation and success in these programs.

Second, workplace discrimination based on criminal

records must be addressed. While certain restrictions may be necessary, such as barring individuals convicted of theft from retail positions, judges could tailor these limitations to the nature of the crime. Broader efforts to eliminate blanket discrimination would enable former inmates to secure meaningful employment and rebuild their lives.

Another critical area of reform beyond the prison system is the policing system. Across the country police departments are underfunded and, in some cases, have become paramilitary organizations with a mandate to combat crime rather than serve and protect—word choice matters. Police are not civilian soldiers holding back evil hordes from raping and pillaging the countryside. Police officers are individuals have chosen to be crisis managers and field technicians for the judicial system. There are times when they are put into danger, but the job is to react to that danger differently than a standard civilian. T

he job is to uphold the letter of law as an exemplar. What does that look like? Officers are mandated to be brave in the face of danger, heroic in the face of disaster, and pinnacles of justice in the face of corruption. In this country, we have all but lost this creed in our police. Police are not trusted. In many circumstances, it appears that they are not trained and equipped to handle danger. Across the country at local, state, and federal levels we must reform police by removing the machismo, ensuring mental health services and screenings, increasing the pay and benefits for officers, increasing their access to training and data driven enforcement techniques, and ensuring that departments across the country have the ethical police forces that are examples of the best citizens a community produces. These reforms will require more funding, and they will require firing and banning a fraction of individuals from being police officers. We have to change the nature of policing in America if we ever hope to have an equitable society of liberty and prosperity.

In summary, the United States must reevaluate its approach to criminal justice. By shifting the focus from punishment to rehabilitation, addressing systemic inequities, fostering opportunities for reintegration, and reforming policing to the noble profession that it once was, society can create a system that truly upholds justice and reduces recidivism. With these kinds of reforms, we can begin to dismantle the cycles of poverty and crime that have long plagued our communities.

Energy and Climate Mitigation

Climate change is undeniably real. The evidence comes from countless sources, whether it's official climate data or simple observations of the world around us. While some argue that climate change is part of a natural cycle, the real question isn't about its origin. Instead, we must focus on how we respond to its impacts, which are already affecting our society in significant ways.

Whether humans caused climate change or not, reducing pollution, using fewer fossil fuels, and adopting sustainable practices are necessary steps. Cutting back on waste, protecting ecosystems, and rethinking agriculture are crucial not only for the environment but also for the health and stability of our species. The goal isn't just to address climate change directly, it's to mitigate its effects and create a sustainable future.

Burning fossil fuels for energy is one of the least efficient uses of this limited resource. Oil has many valuable applications beyond fuel, such as in the production of plastics, medical supplies, and advanced materials. These uses have been crucial to human progress, particularly in healthcare, where sterile environments and lifesaving tools rely on hydrocarbons. By conserving these resources for essential uses, we ensure their availability for future generations. That being said, these materials also have a severe environmental impact. So not only do we need to secure the natural resources that produce the products, but we also need to guarantee that the end of life of these oil products is an environmental net positive.

Switching to renewable energy is critical for both environmental and practical reasons. Fossil fuels are finite, and our reliance on them makes us vulnerable to supply disruptions and price volatility. Events like the COVID-19 pandemic revealed how fragile our current energy systems can be. Transitioning to renewable energy sources like wind, solar, and nuclear power not only reduces our environmental impact but also strengthens energy security. By diversifying our energy infrastructure, we can avoid dependence on unstable global markets and geopolitical conflicts, as seen with Europe's reliance on Russian energy during the Ukraine war.

Renewables also create a more resilient energy grid. Our current systems, built for centralized fossil fuel power, are vulnerable to extreme weather events that are becoming more common. A decentralized, renewable-based grid can withstand these challenges better, ensuring reliable energy even in difficult times.

The future of energy lies in innovation, including breakthroughs like nuclear fusion, which could provide immense energy with minimal environmental impact. To prepare for this future, we must invest in infrastructure now, enabling society to benefit from these advancements when they become available. This point should be underscored. Everything I have proposed is technologically feasible but requires a massive investment in money, manpower, and material. This investment cannot come from the government alone. Therefore, we need public private partnerships where there are significant tax incentives and beneficial financial instruments for fossil fuel dependent companies to make these investments in renewable energy and grid infrastructure. These investments include retraining workforces, improving our energy grid, and building factories for solar panels, wind farms, nuclear power stations, and batteries. It could also include replanting forests and native plants and creating sustainable agriculture operations. We must foster international relationships that ensure access to the minerals and materials needed to accomplish this transformation and the project has to start yesterday.

Addressing climate change is not just about protecting the planet— it's about ensuring humanity's survival. As populations grow, we must find ways to use resources more efficiently. Agriculture, energy, and technology need to adapt to meet rising demands without depleting the environment. Sticking to outdated methods and technologies will only hinder progress.

We are part of nature, not separate from it. To thrive, we must live in harmony with our planet, respecting its limits and adapting to its changes. The choices we make now will determine the future for generations to come. You can make choices today that help this: become vegan or vegetarian, use cold water to wash clothes, avoid buying plastics and consumer items in excess, make electric cars and machines as cool as the internal combustion ones, and support nuclear and renewable energy projects and grid improvements in your backyard. By innovating and evolving, we can secure a better, more sustainable world.

Government Finance and Debt

Every few months, a political battle emerges in American politics over a singular issue that has hindered the progressive agenda for decades. This issue has served as a bludgeon against both Democratic and Republican presidents and candidates alike: ensuring a fiscally responsible government. Reforming this area requires both a philosophical shift and technical changes. Among the proposed measures, the most radical is a vital reform aimed at not only ensuring the longevity of democracy and the strength of the economy but also promoting fairness and equity in economic power, both domestically and globally. This reform strengthens America, and its philosophical foundation is crucial to understanding its significance.

The United States dollar has long been the default

trade currency worldwide. This status is partly due to the U.S. being one of the most productive nations, with a stable currency, government, and fiscal policies. These factors make the U.S. a reliable investment, granting it significant authority in global trade and international relations. Despite this inherent strength, the United States often mismanages its influence, and the debate around fiscal policy reveals stark divides within its political system. Fiscal management remains the primary battleground separating conservatives and liberals.

Conservatives have traditionally emphasized fiscal responsibility, advocating for smaller government and privatization to reduce federal expenditures. However, privatization often diminishes service quality, especially in socially significant areas like prisons and healthcare. The U.S., unlike many nations, operates a largely privatized healthcare system, driven by profit motives, which excludes significant portions of the population from essential services—a moral failing given the country's economic power.

This politicization of fiscal policy has paralyzed effective governance. Sharp divisions often result in a Congress focused solely on temporary budget extensions rather than addressing pressing issues. The slow pace of government reform exacerbates frustrations on government ineptitude and public fear of everything from terrorism to emerging technologies like artificial intelligence. One key source of dysfunction is the debt ceiling, a concept that, though originally intended to ensure fiscal responsibility, has become a recurring crisis point.

The debt ceiling, an arbitrary limit on federal borrowing, fails to serve its purpose. Each year, Congress increases this limit to accommodate the budget, yet the national debt continues to grow. Attempts to manage debt through tax cuts and spending reductions have proven ineffective. Historically, Republican administrations have increased the debt by reducing taxes, while Democratic administrations have moderated the debt by raising taxes. However, structural issues persist, fueled by political gridlock between the executive and legislative branches. This cycle risks government shutdowns, disrupts essential services, and endangers lives.

The proposed reform begins with eliminating the debt ceiling, which is unnecessary from an economic perspective. The ceiling merely serves as a political tool, often to the detriment of effective governance. Instead, we would replace this outdated mechanism with a system of reforms that would actually foster fiscal responsibility. First of all, the Federal Reserve needs to be mandated to tie fiscal policy to nominal GDP, ensuring that physical money supply aligns with economic output. This approach would mitigate inflation and deflation risks, particularly during crises where economic stimulus is needed to ensure basic needs are met. As long as the money supply stays within a margin of nominal GDP, then currency should remain stable.

Another cornerstone of the reform is the establishment of a Governing Fiscal Council comprising representatives from major economic groups, including the Federal Reserve, Treasury Department, Congressional Budget Office, and House and Senate Appropriations Committees. This Council would identify non-negotiable budget items including critical expenditures like debt service payments, core military budgets, federal payrolls, and social safety nets such as Medicare, Medicaid, Social Security, and VA benefits. These items would be funded through tax revenue rather than debt, ensuring fiscal stability.

The Council would also set tax rates within a progressive system, allocating 60% of tax revenue to cover these non-negotiable expenses. Congress would retain control over tax brackets, deductions, and credits, maintaining its legislative power while depoliticizing fiscal management. This structure ensures that core government functions are adequately funded without threatening economic stability.

By eliminating the debt ceiling and creating a Governing Fiscal Council, we would remove the politicization of fiscal policy, prevent government shutdowns, and enable effective governance. Elected officials would still shape fiscal policy through legislative tools, but their actions would no longer jeopardize the nation's economic stability. Debt servicing would take precedence, and tax rates would adjust based on fiscal needs, fostering responsible governance akin to household financial management.

This framework prioritizes economic stability, moral responsibility, and America's global influence. By addressing systemic flaws, it seeks to realign fiscal policy with the principles of equity and functionality, empowering the government to fulfill its obligations to its citizens and reaffirm its position as a responsible global leader.

-Part Three-

WORDS TO ACTION

Alex Hummingbird's Song:

WITHOUT A KING

Hey Ho Gather Round

We are one. We are found

Hey Ho Listen Up

We're not People who give up

Now See everyone

We are different we are one

Now see to the man

We can choose whose in the land

Hey now all of you
Who wish to hate and spew
We now standup strong
To end your terror, right your wrong

Now come one come all
Heres your place to answer the call
Now now all together
Nothing stops us no one's better

O Say can you see
America is here with you and me
O say can't you see
We are only America without a king

Hey now hey now
Don't you fret the road is hard
We're the land of liberty
We fight cause freedom's in our heart

Now I know I know

That the divides seem so apart

But we know we know

We all want equal parts

Hear me true hear me true

The issues aren't so hard

Morally with equity

Our prosperity will start.

O Say can you see

America is here with you and me

O say can't you see

We are only America without a king

Isn't It Too Late?

You can be forgiven, whether you are part of the political mainstream or on its fringes, for believing that debate, voting, and self-governance belong to a bygone era. Perhaps we've fallen too far into oligarchy, institutional decay, and environmental destruction. Maybe America is on its deathbed. To many the grand experiment of the past 250 years seems to be failing. Some argue that we can no longer govern ourselves and that an authoritarian figure is inevitable. All good things must end, right? How could we possibly lift ourselves out of the state of doom we so empirically find ourselves in?

Regardless of political affiliation, this perspective resonates. For some on the conservative side, the country has fallen into immorality, depravity, and corruption, reaching the deepest parts of government institutions. They've lost faith in the legislature, the cabinet, the FBI and every other agency. There are people who have lost faith in the very fabric of truth. To others, the elite few who wield vast wealth, appear to see the world for what it is and want to use their power to shape it according to their will.

Yet here's the reality: if you believe that figures like Donald Trump or Elon Musk—or any powerful oligarch—intend to create a better world for the "little guy," you're hallucinating. History, via Lord Acton, provides the only evidence we need: "absolute power corrupts absolutely." There's no shining example of the rich and powerful turning around to lift up the powerless. That's not how power works nor human nature. America's oligarchs maintain their power through corruption, pollution, dysfunction, war, disease, and division. These are tools wielded to ensure they stay in charge. It is the same playbook from every corner of history most recently Putin's Russia.

But it's also human nature to make change. It is not too late. This country can absolutely self-correct. Change happens when you, me, and 252 million of our friends decide that we've had enough—that we refuse to accept the status quo. At the end of the day, we, the people, hold the power.

If you believe it is too late, you've already lost. Apathy becomes a self-fulfilling prophecy. But this is not a fight rooted in partisanship, nor simply because the alternative might be bad. The fact is history, and current events have shown us what happens under oligarchies and authoritarian rule. Russia is proof enough: the people suffer. The freedoms and quality of life we enjoy in America are products of liberty and democracy, of checks and balances designed to keep power in check so that everyone prospers, including the powerful. Our founders understood that power corrupts, which is why they designed the system the way they did.

We have made it 250 years; there's no reason we cannot make it 250 more. We just have to decide that we want to. We must reject apathy and lies. We must reject leaders who do not lead or solve problems. Anyone who does not meet our standard must go—not through violence, but through collective action. Protest outside their offices until they resign. Challenge them in elections. Vote them out.

There are 252 million eligible voters in this country. Every single one of us can run for office. We could replace our entire government within four years if we chose to. Nothing in America is unfixable. There is no law that says the powerful must always win. In a democracy, the people are the powerful. We must take action in every aspect of our lives. Choose how you raise your children. Choose the companies you support. Choose your leaders and the ideas you want to advance. And if no leader represents your values, then, as Al Gore once said, "be the leader." The most powerful weapon we have is ourselves. We cannot succumb to apathy. We cannot assume that doom is inevitable. That path leads only to tyranny. Instead, we must act—with resolve, perseverance, and a shared commitment to hold ourselves, our neighbors, and our leaders accountable to the values and principles we hold dear.

That is the path to a better world. That is the path to an American utopia.

A Note on the Future of Humanity

This new path for the United States is promising, but America does not exist in a vacuum. Anyone who claims that any country can isolate itself, become entirely self-sufficient, or withdraw from international treaties and global trade is either lying or disastrously naive. Globalization is a bell that cannot be unrung. It has been the trajectory of human civilization for thousands of years.

We like to think that globalization began with the Industrial Revolution, but humanity has been interconnected for far longer. Evidence shows that cultures interacted with one another thousands of years ago. Historical examples, such as the Silk Road and the Roman Empire, illustrate globalization in actionxvi. Believing the US can live in a bubble unto itself or assuming that the framework for a principled republic is applicable only to the United States is shortsighted. Every change we make here, whether toward or away from those principles, sends ripples across the globe.

Though it is sometimes surprising to us insiders, the United States remains a symbol for hope for much of the world. We are seen as a "shining city on a hill" because we are perceived as the first nation to assert that individuals could govern themselves. We are still regarded as a land of opportunity because few other places offer the same level of wealth and social mobility. 250 years of consistent success stories where people find a corner in society, they couldn't find elsewhere are true—but so is our nation's imperfection. The United States leads a world facing grave challenges. We cannot hide behind our own issues and sacrifice a global outlook. Nor can we impose all our values on others.

Certain aspects of liberty, equity, and morality are universally relevant, but these principles must be understood within the 21st-century global context. Humanity has failed to mitigate the worst effects of climate change. Severe weather, rising sea levels, polluted ecosystems, and uninhabitable regions are no longer hypothetical, they are inevitable. Entire coastlines and water supplies are becoming unviable, and climate events like droughts, fires, and desertification are escalating. These phenomena will drive mass migrations, rendering areas around the world, including areas in the United States, inaccessible or uninhabitable.

This is why we need principled immigration policies and frameworks to handle conflicting cultures, shared resources, and the distribution of economic opportunities. We must scale our justice system, immigration programs, and healthcare to ensure we do not fall into a dystopia of lawlessness and chaos. These are not abstract questions or political slogans—they are pressing issues that will shape our daily lives and those of our children and neighbors. We have 10 to 15 years to address them meaningfully, or we risk a chaotic and dysfunctional world.

Humanity's survival is not necessarily in question, but the quality of that survival is. Without decisive action, many people will live in an unfortunate version of the world stripped of prosperity, dignity, and peace. The worst-case scenario does not have to become our reality, but achieving something better requires you adopt two principles:

- ✓ bring solutions, not problems, to every situation
- ✓ respect the dignity and diversity of every human being.

These two ideas can unlock a better future. If every person seeks solutions, collectively, we will find them. If we respect each other as individuals, regardless of differences, we can find common ground in any conflict.

Humanity's diversity is its strength, not a weakness. We may look, sound, and think differently, but we are united by our shared existence on our lone planet and our sacred humanity.

The United States, as a principled republic, has a role to play in shaping this vision. Whether the mantle of leadership remains with us or passes to another nation that embraces these ideals, humanity must strive to respect one another and solve its greatest challenges. Either we find a way forward to a version of utopia, or we face the possibility of a doomful future. The choice is ours. Time is on our side—but only if we act.

What You Can Do

I imagine you're a person of voting age. You may or may not have a job, a family, or a life you find fulfilling. But you still have a very important role as a voter and a member of civilization. If you have made it this far in the book, it means you recognize that problems exist—in this country and in the world—and you have the desire to do something about it. So, what is that something? There are three things every person can do to ensure progress: learn, exercise compassion and trust, and make your voice heard.

1. Learn

We cannot operate as a functioning society if we are uninformed. So, learn everything you can—be curious. Especially when it comes to political issues, you have more access to information than any generation before you. Not just the basics but the nuances of complex topics can be found and explained in a way you can understand. In reality, you don't need to become an expert in everything, but you can at least know enough to identify nonsense when you hear it.

That said, misinformation thrives in today's media landscape. The great thing about misinformation, though, is that it will never stand up to verification. So, keep asking "why" and continue questioning what you're told. Seek multiple sources—trust those that are reputable, like encyclopedias, peer-reviewed journals, universities, and local newspapers. Obviously, news media organizations often have agendas, so always take what you hear with a grain of salt. But compare what you hear from one outlet with other outlets and reputable sources. The truth will always become apparent when you seek it. But remember you have to be open to the truth, even if it is against your beliefs, your dogmas, your instincts, and your desires. Truth does not care about you or what you think; facts are omnipresent and indelible.

2. Exercise Compassion and Trust

There are always going to be people who disagree with you. Understand this: people form their opinions about the world and politics because of their unique experiences and perspectives. Respect that. Your perspective brought you to your opinion, and their perspective brought them to theirs.

Even if those who disagree with you are part of the MAGA Oligarchy, or a sect of Antifa Anarcho-feminists, they themselves are not the root of the problem. The leaders of that movement, which directly benefit from having power, are the real problem. Everyday people, even those who strongly disagree with you, are processing the world through a different lens. If you approach conversations with compassion and respect for their humanity, you'll discover that compromise is possible. If you can find common ground with someone else, then so can everyone.

To that end, trust also matters — trust in the process and trust in institutions. Are there people in those institutions who are corrupt? Of course. But if you write off an entire organization, department, or group of people as broken or irredeemable, you're only helping the corrupt maintain their grip. We must believe that institutions can work, though they may need reform.

No government program, organization, or individual is perfect; everything is a work in progress. But what we can and must demand is accountability. Institutions are not some amorphous, faceless blobs. They are people with lives and children and pains and hobbies who are trying their hardest, even if their best is not always good enough. The organization can always be improved, but we must remember that it is still people at its core.

3. Make Your Voice Heard

This starts with voting in every single election and on every single item on the ballot. Understand what you're voting for and make an informed decision. I am not here to advocate for any one party or position. What matters is that your decisions are based on facts and critical thought—what you truly believe will make the world better. If everyone votes according to what they genuinely think is best, we'll already be on the path to a better society.

But voting is not enough. You also need to speak out. Write to your elected officials. Let them know where you stand. Engage in conversations with those around you, even those who disagree, and work toward compromise. Use your voice to call for change, to challenge leaders, and to hold everyone accountable, including yourself.

By learning, showing compassion, trusting the process, and making your voice heard, you will become part of the solution. The problems of this world are vast, but no problem is insurmountable when people are willing to act.

As an aside, some of you will be in positions of immense power as corporate leaders, influencers, officials, and personalities. There is immense pressure to maintain a status quo that has created genuine prosperity for you, your friends, and those you work for. I cannot begrudge your desire to keep the system. But you will be on the wrong side of history. The only universal law in human civilization is that we are constantly evolving towards a freer, more equitable, and more tolerant society. You can choose personal prosperity over the betterment of lives in this generation and those that come. Or you can choose to be a part of the solution. You prosper no matter what. So why not be generous with your power? There are no rules in life, only decisions and consequences. You have the capacity to create a new paradigm that is a win-win for everyone. You get that privilege because you have privilege. I have privilege and choose to use it. The people that history remembers have always made the same decision. Will you?

To Politicians With Love

Let's speak plainly. A real leader is not just a politician prattling for soundbites or clutching at power. Real leaders are the ones willing to take the hits, stand on principle, and push for a society that reflects what we all deserve: equity, liberty, and morality. Those three words—simple enough—are not just ideals we hang on the wall. They are the foundation of what makes a society just. As a political leader, whether elected, appointed or hired, you have unique power to influence society to measure up to that vision. There are four rules of political engagement that you should pledge to if you want to be someone that helps create a utopia.

1. Stop playing Small

Too many political leaders are afraid of rocking the boat. They dance around the edges of issues, focused on the next election cycle, the next headline, the next donor check. Too many times, we have seen presidential debates where the only answers are non-answers. Actually, answer the question and you will see your poll numbers go up. But you can not fix a sinking ship by pretending it is not taking on water. Leaders need the guts to call things what they are. Inequity? Name it. Corruption? Call it out. Injustice? Root it out. Because progress doesn't happen when people in power whisper the truth behind closed doors. It happens when they stand in front of all of us, say it loudly, and act on it. And if the other guy is yelling a false truth, yell louder. That is your mandate.

2. Build Policies Around Equity - Not Equality

I have discussed this over and over throughout this work, but you have the option to act on this right now so I will say it again. Equity recognizes that not everyone starts from the same place. A real leader understands this. They're not afraid to ask, "What does fairness actually look like?" Answer this not in a broad, blanket sense, but in a way that acknowledges the lived realities of people who have been left behind—economically, racially, geographically.

It's not enough to give everyone the same tools if some are starting three steps behind. Political leaders must create policies that lift people up to a level playing field—not policies that pat themselves on the back for "equal access" when half the room can not reach the door.

3. Liberty requires Guardrails

Liberty is fundamental, but liberty without responsibility is chaos. As a leader, your job is to thread that needle. You need to recognize that liberty is not just about the freedom to act, but also about freedom from harm—freedom from exploitation, poverty, violence, and discrimination. Liberty means creating an environment where people are free to thrive. That requires laws and systems that protect the vulnerable while holding the powerful accountable. The guardrails are necessary, and leaders who pretend otherwise are selling a lie. Choose not to be that guy.

4. Morality Is About Action Not Words

The word 'morality' gets thrown around a lot. Everyone claims they have it, but fewer are willing to put it into practice when it's inconvenient. Real morality means centering human dignity in every decision. It's making the hard call to do what's right, even when it's unpopular. It's standing up for the people who do not have a voice: the poor, the sick, the marginalized, the forgotten. As a leader, you must be held to a moral standard, not a political one. And that moral standard should always ask: "Does this decision honor people? Does it make their lives better, freer, fairer?" If the answer is no, it's the wrong decision.

5. Be a Builder, Not a Divider

It's easy to tear things down. It's easy to point fingers, stir anger, and exploit division to maintain power. But that's not leadership. Leaders build. They build coalitions. They build trust. They build systems that work for everyone. They don't lead by fear; they lead by vision. If you can't inspire people to believe in something bigger than their differences, you are not leading. You are taking up space, resources, and time. Please step aside.

At the end of the day, as a political leader you owe it to the people you serve to act boldly, honestly, and with an unshakable sense of purpose. A principled society—a society that champions equity, liberty, and morality—does not emerge by accident. It's built brick by brick, policy by policy, decision by decision, by leaders who know that their power is not a privilege. It's a responsibility. And if they are not up for that responsibility, they need to get out of the way. The rest of us have a world to rebuild.

Acknowledgements

First of all, I would like to thank my family, my dad and my sister, for their eternal love and support. Creating this work and whatever things come out of it would not be possible without you. Particularly to my dad, and to my mother, I want to thank you for the way that you raised me. You gave me opportunities to learn, you ensured I went to incredible schools, and the foundation of education and curiosity that you built has made this possible. To my sister, Kyla, you have been indispensable in helping me shape this work. It is you who I have in mind as my audience and your editing skills have helped make this work functional.

To my girlfriend Courtney, you have been a light in my life since we met. You inspire me with your support and your affection. The strength and permission to be myself is a powerful fuel that has been used throughout to make this work happen.

To friends and colleagues who I have known, you are my teachers. Brittany L., Chantal C., Kevin D., Walter K., Danny L., Dulce J., Bella B., Greg H., Craig A, Nate L. and I'm sure many others—you have shaped me to who I am, given me perspective, and love. I would not have been able to make this work without the experiences I had at Johns Hopkins University, with JHU Black student union, and ASA clubs. I would not have had this perspective without studying abroad at FAMU and the many conversations with Jan. I want to thank influencers who know nothing about me but who have created me: Malcolm Gladwell, Jon Stewart, John Oliver, Walter Isaacson, Wes Moore, George Will, Kara Swisher, Scott Galloway, Robert Reich, Bernie Sanders, Daniel Goleman, Barack Obama, and many others. I stand on the shoulders of giants.

Endnotes

i Objective Morality is a combination of various philosophical treatments. Jean-Jacque Rouseaus's The Social Contract and John Stuart Mill's On Liberty are significant influences. Also I learned about Jesuit concept of casuistry from Malcolm Gladwell's podcast Revisionist History which has influenced by sense of secular humanism which I've read about at the website for the American Humanist Society. Additionally, one of the most important influences for my understanding of morality came from the understanding that babies have an innate sense of morality. I first encountered that idea in documentary many years ago. Researchers like Paul Bloom and Melanie Killen have pioneered the concept. Finally ideas from Ayn Rand, Isaac Asimov, and Gene Roddenberry have informed my philosophical leans. All of these influences have combined to form what I call Objective Morality.

ii I am a natural student of history and have long been fascinated by the changing winds of economic and political philosophy. My understanding of Reagans' influence comes from documentaries such as the "Untold History of the United States" by Oliver Stone and CNN's "The 80s." I learned a lot about how 1980s economic policies in the US and UK created ripple effects for decades from the nonfiction book Stolen by Grace Blakeley. I've discussed these topics with my father extensively as he was there. I have read about conservative and republican party history and economic theories from George Will when he was still with the National Review. Two specific pop culture references sparked my interest in learning about the legacy of Reagan's presidency. First, in his album To Pimp a Butterfly Kendrick Lamar makes references to how Reaganomics and his drug policies contributed to the high incarceration rates and poverty in Compton. Secondly, the Adam McKay's movie Vice he discusses Steve Atwater and other key conservative figures that started in Nixon's White house but found their influence in Reagan's error. I synthesize all of this into the most critical insight for this context -- that Reagan's 'trickle down economics' was a horrendous political tool to justify anarcho-capitalist policies to working class people. But those policies largely gutted the middle class, destroyed unions, and imbalanced the power dynamics between consumers and corporations. These impacts are still felt today especially since my conservative politicians still use similar arguments.

iii This concept of grading society based on how well it balances social needs comes from enlightenment philosophy such as Jean-Jacque Rousseau, John Locke, and John Stuart Mill. This comes from the same intellectual and philosophical DNA that lead to me Objective Morality.

iv A significant part of my understanding of American Revolutionary history comes from reading Walter Isaacson's Benjamin Franklin biography. It is a deeply insightful work that gives an excellent perspective on the structure of the colonial government, the grievances of the colonists, and their efforts to create a better life for themselves. Franklin was intricately involved in all aspects of this history.

v Jefferson, T. (2024). Declaration of Independence. Retrieved from National Archives: https://www.archives.gov/founding-docs/declaration-transcript

vi Amanat, A. (2018). Iran A Modern History. Yale University Press. This history of Iran provides an incredible window in Persian history but also gives insights into topics such as the relationship between government and religion. Among the important lessons that Iran's history gives us is how powerful religion can be in a non-secular society both as fuel for power and a force of chaos.

vii. My understand of abortion comes from years of being a democrat and hearing the stories and reports about the issue. I do not have a religious background, so those kinds of perspectives have never resonated with me but the science of the process and sociological factors with the practice have been deeply interesting to me. On a personal, I have had close personal friends who have gone through this decision. I have sat with my friend while making this decision and experienced the emotional turmoil that resulted.

viii. My understanding of American history in this context comes from a strong high school education, documentaries such as Oliver Stone's Untold History of the United States and Ken Burns' Civil War. I have completed a seminars on racism and racial history, educated myself on critical race theory, and continue to have a passion for history through works such as Walter Isaacson's Benjamin Franklin.

ix Paine, T. (1776). Common Sense. Boston.

x Adelman, L. (Director). (2003). Race the Power of an Illusion [Motion Picture].

xi The Constitution of the United States. (2025). Retrieved from National Archives: https://www.archives.gov/founding-docs/constitution

xii Schenck V US, 249 US 47 (1919) (US Supreme Court 1919). Retrieved from https://www.oyez.org/cases/1900-1940/249us47

xiii Burns, K. (Director). (1990). Civil War [Motion Picture]. Additionally, this is a subject that I was taught about extensive in my high school US history class. There is a common misunderstanding – largely due to poorly taught high school history – which surmises that the civil war was a kind race war. The issue was not racism but slavery as an economic modality and specifically, who had power to regulate that modality- the federal government or states themselves.

xiv Holland, L., & Schumacher, P. (2024). Giving or Getting? New York's Balance of Payments with the Federal Government (2024). SUNY Rockefeller Institute of Government. Retrieved from https://rockinst.org/issue-area/new-yorks-balance-of-payments-with-the-federal-government-2024/

xv Kurzweil, R. (2005). The Singularity is Near. New York: Penguin Books.

xvi My understanding of the history of political discourse, communication, information, and its relationship with the industrial revolution and technological change is something I've learned about from multiple sources. In high school, I took a course called AP Human Geography which is an incredible powerful survey of the forces and influences on human society spanning history. This course included topics from religion and government to nature of prisons and contributions of agriculture and other technologies for human development. Furthermore, I have experienced lectures on Wondrium from professors such a Dr. Vejas Gabriel Liulevicius. This combined with readings from Ray Kurzweil, Noam Chomsky, Walter Isaacson, and I'm sure others have given me a diverse picture of history and the interconnectedness of technology and social change.

xvii Briton, M. (2022). The Estonian Miracle: E-Estonia and the Future of Digital Infrastructure. https://www.sps.nyu.edu/homepage/metaverse/metaverse-blog/the-estonian-miracle-e-estonia-and-the-future-of-digital-infrastructure.html: NYU.

xviii I have a deep understanding of socialist and communist structures. First of all, I have learned the American history of socialism such as about Eugene Debs from lecture series and documentaries. Secondly, I have read the Communist Manifesto by Karl Marx and some other essays by Engels. I learned a lot of soviet society and communism while living in Prague for study abroad during my undergraduate studies in 2016. Finally, on China in particular, the Guardian put out a series in the late 2010s (I couldn't find the specific set of articles). Nonetheless this series delve deep into the historical and political events and structure that govern Chinese society and the economy. They explained the hybrid communo-capitalist system that China uses. Over the years, I have read similar accounts about how business, especially for international companies like Tesla and Apple, do business in China.

xix O'Dell, H. (2024, April 10). Multiple countries have tested a universal basic income – and it works. Retrieved from Blue Marble: https://globalaffairs.org/bluemarble/multiple-countries-have-tested-universal-basic-income-and-it-works

xx My understanding of the healthcare industry comes from several sources. First of all, my first exposure to the business model and challenges of the pharmaceutical industry was in 2017 when I was videographer for the Gap Summit at Georgetown University which featured speakers in biomedical research and pharmaceuticals. I absorbed a lot from watching the panels at that conference, talking with some of the participants, and editing those segments into YouTube content. Additionally, in 2022 I started working as a product owner and business intelligence engineer for a psychiatry firm that was building an Electronic Health Records system. I went on to also work as a product owner for another Electronic Health Records SaaS company. Over this period of about 2 years, I was given a crash course in how the health care business actually works from operational challenges, to billing procedures, financial challenges, and the daily struggles of practitioners and patients. In these roles, it was my job to find solutions to many of these problems which meant that I came to understand these problems very deeply.

xxi As a result of my father having diabetes and my goals for having an extraordinarily long life, I have been a nerd about learning about health and nutrition. We have watched numerous documentaries on the subjects such as What the Health, What's with Wheat, and The Gamechangers. Also, I have read and watched documentaries that discuss the details of How Not to Die by Dr Michael Greger. These sources have contributed to my opinions on preventative care, the Food to Pharma Pipeline and other issues.

xxii On a personal note, I have worked with my father for years to get his insurance needs met. He was self-employed, then unemployed, and ultimately now is disabled. So, we have gone through the ACA marketplaces, dealt with Medicaid in 3 states, Medicare, Medicare Advantage Plans, and I've had private insurances myself through my work. Navigating all of this has given me a rather jaded perspective on the convoluted and deeply flawed structure that these programs operate in. My experience in working in healthcare billing only adds to it because frankly, the doctors, hospitals, and administrators are doing what they must- it's the system itself that is flawed.

www.ingramcontent.com/pod-product-compliance
Lightning Source LLC
Chambersburg PA
CBHW060419130626
46555CB00005B/2128
* 9 7 9 8 9 9 2 9 6 8 7 3 6 *